CAN YOU TOLERATE THIS? *ESSAYS*

ASHLEIGH YOUNG

CAN YOU TOLERATE THIS?

ESSAYS

BLOOMSBURY PUBLISHING
LONDON • OXFORD • NEW YORK • NEW DELHI • SYDNEY

BLOOMSBURY PUBLISHING
Bloomsbury Publishing Plc
50 Bedford Square, London, WC1B 3DP, UK

BLOOMSBURY, BLOOMSBURY PUBLISHING and the Diana logo are trademarks of
Bloomsbury Publishing Plc

This book, in different form, was originally published in New Zealand by
Victoria University Press, 2016
First published in Great Britain 2018

The following essays were previously published, in different form:
'Black Dog Book' in *Sport*; 'Wolf Man' in *Landfall*; 'Katherine Would Approve' in *Five Dials*;
'Sea of Trees' in *Griffith Review*; 'Anemone' in *Tell You What: Great New Zealand
Nonfiction 2017*, edited by Susanna Andrew and Jolisa Gracewood (Auckland University Press).

The author gratefully acknowledges permission to reprint: Frank O'Hara, excerpts from
'Adieu to Norman, Bon Jour to Joan and Jean-Paul', from *Lunch Poems*. Copyright 1954 by
Frank O'Hara. Reprinted with the permission of The Permissions Company, Inc., on behalf of
City Lights Books, www.citylights.com.

All of JP Young's lyrics and correspondence are reprinted with his kind permission.

A catalogue record for this book is available from the British Library

ISBN: HB: 978-1-5266-0035-6; eBook: 978-1-5266-0037-0

2 4 6 8 10 9 7 5 3 1

Book design by Lauren Kolm and Greg Heinimann
Printed and bound in Great Britain by CPI Group (UK) Ltd, Croydon CR0 4YY

To find out more about our authors and books visit www.bloomsbury.com
and sign up for our newsletters

for Ngaire and Kiwa

contents

bones

It stands silently and elegantly and reveals
its secrets if you ask the right questions.
—*Dr. Frederick S. Kaplan, orthopedic surgeon,
authority on fibrodysplasia ossificans progressiva,
1998*

Harry's first skeleton was the one he was born with. That was the healthy skeleton of a small boy. The only odd thing about this skeleton was that it had a bulbous bony protrusion on the left big toe; aside from that it was ordinary. His bones were ordinary bones: they were made of living cells and had marrow inside them, like the bones of fish, birds, mammals. There's a photograph of Harry as a six-year-old, wearing shorts and a T-shirt, knobbly-kneed, with a lopsided smile and sticky-out ears. His blond hair is roughed up like he's just come in from running around or riding a bike outside with his sister Helene.

It was around the time of this photograph that a second skeleton began to grow around Harry's first skeleton. This bone, too, was ordinary bone. But it was heterotopic: in another place, the wrong place. The only time in our lives that ossification—the transformation of cartilage into bone—should occur is when we are inside the womb. No new bones are supposed to grow once a person is born. They are supposed to be whole then. But it was as if this second skeleton of Harry's was working to shelter the first, as if the first was too fragile to continue going along on its own. If Harry hurt himself—if he broke his leg or stubbed his toe—his body repaired itself by growing bone in the place where he had been hurt. It took a few days or weeks for the bone to appear. The only way his body knew how to heal was to harden, so afraid it seemed of leaving any part of him vulnerable.

There are four further photographs of Harry, all of them medical photographs taken in front of a blank wall, and in all of them Harry is in his underwear so that the form of his body can be clearly documented. At nine years old he is still smiling, and he seems braced in position by choice; his slightly crooked stance makes him look mischievous, like any nine-year-old. This is the last photograph in which he is able to raise his head to look directly at the camera. At eleven, thirteen, and twenty he is curved. Something seems to ripple in bigger and bigger waves under his skin. His eyes are lowered to his hands, as if he is concentrating on getting himself out of handcuffs.

As stark as these photographs are, they also show grace.

Harry looks poised, as if about to raise his arms above his head and pirouette. His head and torso curve to the left, a delicate bow. Even as he is wracked and pushed about by his new skeleton, he flows.

Whenever Harry's physicians cut the new skeleton away, it would grow back forcefully over the next few months, as if in a panic. Soon it bound him tightly. Bone covered his back like a cracking cocoon. It welded his upper arms to his breastbone so that his arms hovered magician-like in front of his body. Bone wrapped itself in layers around his skull. Delicate columns of bone, like stalactites, fused his head to his neck, forcing him to stare at the ground. One of his legs was bent back, as if he were forever about to kick a ball, as if all the world were waiting in a grandstand around him. He could still move about by shuffling along with a cane. But when he was twenty, when his mother could no longer care for him, he went to live at a nursing home in Philadelphia called the Philadelphia Home for Incurables.

In his thirties, ossification reached Harry's lower jaw, which became locked to his skull, leaving him unable to speak. He couldn't brush his teeth, cough, stick out his tongue, lick an envelope or his own lips, whistle, or eat. He lay in bed at the home, a diagram of himself, as if his second skeleton wanted to fuse him to a single spot and keep him safe there. He should never move haphazardly through the world like others did.

It was six days before his fortieth birthday that Harry died. His physicians took his body, as Harry himself had wished: bequeathing it to science would give meaning and depth to medical and scientific research on FOP for decades. Following on from the few photographs of Harry as a boy and a young man, there are many, many photographs—from all angles and proximities—depicting only his skeleton.

He stands today in the Mütter Museum of the College of Physicians in Philadelphia, the city in which he was born. He's not far from the plaster death cast of Chang and Eng, the conjoined twin brothers who died in 1874, aged sixty-two. In life, a seven-inch-long ligament joined them at the chest. The liver they shared is displayed beside them in a glass jar, preserved in formalin.

Harry is alone inside a glass case. He stands on one leg, as he stood in life, his other leg bent behind him. He was easy to put together. Ordinary human skeletons require fine wires and glue for articulation—the gentle drawing upward of the bones, so that they hold together and stand tall. Without the wires and glue, they tumble into a pile. Harry's skeleton stood tall without help, because the plates, sheets, ribbons, and thorns of his second skeleton fused him almost completely into one piece. You wouldn't know Harry's face or his handwriting or the sound of his voice, but even though he is faceless and silent, left alone he is self-supporting and strong. We can look on the contained explosion of his skeleton, the way it seems forever breaking but never broken. Physicians, scientists, and students return and return to it; they say he is their Sphinx. Harry's sister Helene comes each year to see him too, and to pay her respects.

witches

Each of us begins in the nude, it's true. In most of those early photographs we are naked—wandering around the neighbor's backyard with a bucket, sitting in a river looking up, waving through an open window. It seems expected of us to be in the nude. Our legs are bandy and soft. Our arms are rolls of fat. Our face doesn't yet belong to us; all we really own are our eyes. We are greedy with them—we look and look, gobbling up our parents and brothers and pets with our eyes, looking at everything but ourselves. The self is a place where things are got—food, touch, sleep—and our conviction is that the world exists to give things to us. We call that world into being each time we open our eyes.

We laugh now about how unself-conscious we were then, how easy it was to be in the nude. There are photographs of us running naked, hands bunched as we tilt forward, amazed. We don't remember being amazed. We don't remember arriving in a doorway naked and glaring up at a taller person who must have raised a camera to her face.

At some point in memory, days begin to grow out of fragments. The days sharpen and become facts. Always this point is during summer at the sea, when our hunger rose up cleanly inside our stomach, like a rock out of the water, and we weren't afraid to swim out to it—we ate and ate. "It's the sea air," said our mother, stroking our arms and our brother's at the same time. Many arms stretched toward her. Our arms were long and thin and covered in soft blond hair like thistledown. Our fingers seemed prehensile. Our arms and hands grew at a much faster rate than the rest of us, as if forever reaching out to be stroked. By the time we were eight years old, our arms hung halfway down our legs.

What became of our friend? We had one special friend who came with us on holidays, she and her older sister. We sat with our friend on the banks of the lagoon beside a mangled tree stump, which was our boat or our horse for riding over crabs at low tide. Naked, we crouched on the beach and scooped the sand out of the lagoon bank. Using our shoulders and forearms, we dug handful after handful and smoothed it over our arms and legs, over our faces and into our hair, slowly charring ourselves black, a game we called Witches. We ladled a large silken scoop onto our heart and watched it drift down our chest and belly and between our legs. Postcard-neat: legs splayed in front of us, charred peninsulas.

The beach is uncompromised by memory. The streams that ran into our lagoon had pretty scalloped edges. The farther inland the streams ran, the slower the water moved and the darker the sand became, until it had the greenish tinge of frog skin. It was a rough beach, with dinosaur bones of wood lying all around the river mouth, where the water moved too fast to cross, and mohawks of flax growing all over the hills. The beach belonged to us in a way that no place has belonged to us since, in a way no city or town can belong to us. We have decided never to go back to this beach because it will have changed beyond the memory, and this will be distressing, or it will be empty and this will be worse. The lagoon gone, signposts now only posts, cabins lifted away to reveal crabgrass threadbare in the sand. The sea replaced with a thinning tarpaulin held down by rocks.

We remember our friend's skin: salamander skin. All over she was smooth and hairless, with a white belly, dimply bottom, and feet that banged the ground. When she ran indoors the furniture rattled, and her mother would look up from her book and cigarette, murmuring gently about the need to slow down, sit still, please . . . Our friend would assume a terrible silence, then the storm would come. *Shut up, get lost, you're all bastards and bitches.* Sometimes she would hit both her parents and they would grip her arms and hold on tight as if keeping her from blowing away. We watched these exchanges with fear and admiration. What would happen if we behaved like this? We felt excited in advance.

We looked forward to turning into a teenager, when we would be entitled to shout and slam doors and be hated by our parents.

Our friend was covered in faint gold freckles, as if she'd grown on a tree. Her hair was a thin orange. Ours was mousy, and in winter it was coarse and dark. Our mother called it golden, but in our heart we knew. On the beach it didn't matter. In our witch costume we looked the same as our friend, with our black sand hair and black-rimmed fingernails. We reclined with our friend on the sand: two stinking seals, barking with laughter.

We know of no other time in our life when our body felt this inconsequential. Our arms and legs were light because our bones were hollow. Our body knew two states best, moving fast and lying still; it had no use for anything else. We could have lain right in the middle of the beach, camouflaged in the sand, and no one would have glanced at us. Only our blinking eyes might have given us away, but they could have passed for shells, especially our friend's, which were the shining gray-blue of paua. Ours, of course, were the color of snails.

We can't pinpoint a moment when we learned that the nakedness could not go on, the moment when we looked down at our body and saw what it was. We tell ourselves now that it must have been a gradual change. It must have been a creeping awareness of temperature and shadow and weight, in the same way that the cold comes on when the sun drops behind the sea: a soft gray net comes down. We must have begun to look at our body, to find it from the corners of our eyes to see if it moved differently under our watch. It did. Our body walked too quickly, as though a tailwind were pressing it forward, and then sometimes very early in the morning it turned into the clay beneath sand

and paralyzed us, and a second body sat on our chest. At night our body walked around, taking us outside to the woodpile or to the foot of our parents' bed, where we woke to find ourselves deep in conversation. Our body tried to fold up at the first sign of danger, as if disappearing into a shell, not realizing that the shell, too, was our body, that it was a thing both apart from and forever clinging to our backs.

There must have been a last time, even if we didn't know it then. We must have stood up on the beach, covered in sand, and felt suddenly heavy, as if wearing many layers of petticoats. Immediately the sand began to slide down our skin, and we'd have known that soon it would become lace. Our friend was laughing. The measure of a person was how funny they were, and our reaction was always to laugh too, helplessly. The black sand made the openings of her face seem new: her mouth as pink as a conch, her eyes lashless; she was as if smoothed by many years of wind and rain and sand. Perhaps it was then that we became afraid she was looking at us, our body showing too much through the sand. So we started running.

We must have felt our sand costume lifting and falling around us, pattering behind our feet, our witch skirts clinging to our legs. Rings of sand flew off our fingers. By the time we finally tipped into the water, our costume was almost gone, but then it must have lifted away completely. We felt it lift and become a cloud in the water. Our eyes opened. As soon as we came to the surface, we would be faced with the question of how to get back to the cabins and tents without being seen. We stayed under the water for as long as possible, holding our breath tight like a fist, fighting our buoyancy.

the te kūiti underground

It seems to me that the realest reality lives
somewhere beyond the edge of human vision.
—*Russell Hoban*

Halfway up View Road, I turned to look back the way I had come. View Road was a gravel road, a dead end. Below me was a crosshatching of fields and roads and the sewage pond, and you could see the airport in my hometown, Te Kūiti. The airport wasn't really an airport at all but a strip of mown grass with poplar trees at each end and a tumbledown house, the clubhouse, where the pilots, including my father, gathered. It was really just another field, the planes like large animals.

As I stood looking, catching my breath, a young man appeared around the corner about a hundred meters away. I felt a small leap in my chest. He'd been following me, I thought. Looking for me. He'd had a hunch I would be out walking alone, as I often was, and now here he was. I heard the crunch of his boots on the gravel as he approached. Perhaps I should have turned and walked away, avoiding his eyes, but I stayed very still. The man was wearing a gray T-shirt, the collarless sort with a few buttons below the neck. Straight-legged blue jeans. He was also wearing sandals, which was a bit unusual. As he got closer he raised his eyebrows and made a slight pout, and, I swear, his head wobbled a bit from side to side. He reached for my hand. Yes. It was Paul McCartney.

Specifically, it was Paul McCartney as he appeared in his picture in the liner notes of *The White Album*: unshaven, almost disheveled-looking. His fringe was just riffling his eyebrows; his eyes were a sad liquid. Together we began to walk, hand in hand. I noted that Paul McCartney's fingers were slightly callused. Of course: he'd just finished playing the bass on the greatest album of all time. We walked slowly to the top of View Road, then we looked out at the hills, trees, roads, cows, the interlocking parts of nowhere. We talked about music, books, writing, our families. I had a lot to say to Paul but much of it wasn't ready to form words, so it filled my chest like a balloon. Still, Paul looked at me sideways, nodding in agreement as I didn't talk.

It was 1997. The Beatles had split nearly thirty years before. In this reality, Paul McCartney's face was beginning its slow collapse. Anyone coming the other way on View Road, not that there was ever anyone, would have seen a grim-faced girl with her hand flapping out at one side as she walked.

As my favorite bands changed, Paul became mutable. He would start out as Paul and on the way home become George. A few times he was Tom Petty, wearing a black hat, then Billy Corgan, scowling attractively, before he lost his hair. For a good long while he was Thom Yorke, his lazy eye fluttering in the harsh light. And soon he was Beck too, loping along in sneakers and acid-washed jeans, occasionally shrieking with laughter like he did on *Mellow Gold*. It was enough to imagine a warm, intelligent presence, but this presence was always a musician from a stage or studio in a big city from somewhere in the world. It was always someone who could make an ordinary place, an ordinary moment, more intense, more like a film, something driven toward meaningful conclusion.

I'd told myself stories before and sometimes written them down, before sending them off to the editor of the *New Zealand School Journal*, whose address I'd copied from the inside cover of one of the volumes at school. There was a hedgehog, I wrote, that went hang gliding off the top of Mangarino Road. There was an intricate messaging system among the tiny crayfish in the streams in the wilderness above our house. Aliens had crash-landed their UFO in the trees and now had a secret colony there! My stories received polite rejection letters from the editor of the *School Journal*, which I showed my parents with sorrow. But I was fourteen now and wanted to be part of the story. I wanted to walk beside someone from a different universe, someone who would turn Te Kūiti into something else. Its army-blanket green would become a romantic backdrop, the way the desert was a romantic backdrop in *The English Patient*, instead of just lonely and hostile.

At the same time, the landscape of Te Kūiti created a delicious sadness in me. The hills, the row of pines above a clay bank, the Te Kūiti sky, a smothering gray—these surroundings confirmed and enhanced my loneliness, showed me that it was real. I didn't have many friends at high school, I didn't have a boyfriend, and although I wanted to be a writer, I wanted more to be in a band and become very famous. I had a limited sense of the ridiculous but a strong sense of the melodramatic, and I gathered the landscape into my mood as if gathering up a luxurious fabric, pulling it round me and breathing it in. I believed that no one living in Te Kūiti had ever felt the same as I felt then.

One day I wrote a fan letter to Beck, whose album *Odelay* had just arrived at the CD store on Rora Street. "Dear Beck, I have never written a fan letter before"—this, of course, was a lie; I had written to many famous people, including Paul McCartney— "but I wanted to write to say how much I love *Odelay*." I imagined Beck reading the letter, slightly distracted at first and then drawn in by my words, marveling that his music had traveled all the way to the bottom of the world to a girl who lived in a town he would never have known existed, if not for my letter.

A few weeks, perhaps a month later, I received a reply from Beck. Or from someone pretending to be him. The letter said:

"Wow, what's it like living in New Zealand? Do y'all have the Funky Chicken there?—Beck." I read the letter over and over, my hands shaking, until it ceased to make sense. Although, I had to admit, the letter hadn't made much sense from the start. What was the Funky Chicken? Was it a dance, a food, a fast food joint? What amazed me was not just that Beck had written back to me. It was that he had written the words "New Zealand." He'd spoken the secret code that granted us access to the rest of the world. And he was interested to know what it was like here. It didn't seem an idle interest, but a genuine one. He'd said "Wow."

I wrote a long letter in reply. No, as far as I knew we didn't have the Funky Chicken; what was it exactly? I told him about my town, how its closest city was Hamilton, and that every year we had a celebration called Midnight Madness, when all the shops stayed open till midnight, and there was a sheep-shearing competition at the Civic Centre. Te Kūiti men were so fast at shearing, I told Beck, that the town was known as the Shearing Capital of the World. I wrote about this mockingly, as if talking about someone in my class at school who I'd decided was a moron. I told him that the Mangaokewa River often flooded and made the riverbank muddy so I couldn't walk my dog there. I also told him in some detail about walking up View Road and imagining him walking with me, in his checked shirt and jeans and old sneakers, the same outfit he'd worn in that interview in *Spin* magazine.

I didn't hear from Beck again. But the first letter made me feel that I was destined for great things.

. . .

As I played the piano and howled into the living room, singing about the broken heart I hadn't yet experienced, I sometimes thought about being on a stage with my brother JP. It was JP who was becoming famous. He was doing a songwriting course in Hamilton and he had a four-track recording machine. He'd had a song on student radio and he regularly played gigs with his band, the Clampers, who had a small but devoted following in Hamilton.

To my father, JP's pursuit of a career in music was baffling. Nobody made any money writing songs, certainly nobody who came from a town of farmers, electricians, and accountants like him. "You've got to have money coming in," he told my brother. "You can't not have money coming in." In secret, JP and I made fun of this belligerence. *Gotta have money coming in. Gotta have money coming in.* It became a kind of chant.

Despite this, I knew that Dad liked to hear JP play. He would cajole him into playing at birthday parties. (Sometimes JP would impersonate Dad: "'Play some Eagles, JP. They'll love it. Play "Hotel California"!' I feel like a performing monkey.") When JP relented and got out his guitar, Dad looked as happy as I'd ever seen him. Leaning on the bar, awkward with pride. We were all proud, though in my case envious too, when JP auditioned to play at a Neil Finn and Friends concert in Hamilton and was chosen to play alongside the man himself—Neil Finn, the great Neil Finn, of Split Enz and Crowded House. There was a photo in the *Waikato Times* of the two of them standing on the stage, looking uncannily like brothers: blond hair, long arms, guitars held at the same angle. JP is mid-song, wide-eyed in the expensive-looking spotlight. He looks braced, maybe hitting a high note. Neil Finn is holding out one hand toward him as if presenting JP to the world.

When JP came home to Te Kūiti for the occasional weekend or at term break, Dad sometimes cornered him in the kitchen. "I was talking to a bloke at Omya," he might begin. Omya was the limeworks across the railway line from the airport, a place of blinding white gravel and cooling towers and mini forklift trucks constantly in reverse. "I thought we could set something up." He would look at JP with a funny expression, leaving the words on the brink: *Gotta have money coming in.* We'd all stand there in the kitchen, Dad in his office clothes, me in my high-school uniform, Mum in an apron with her glass of Country cask wine, and JP in his cardigan and cord pants, plumes of blond hair sticking up around his head. He'd been writing songs all day and recording them in the bathroom, where the acoustics were better. "All right, I'll have a think about it," he'd say unhappily. Many of the worst jobs he ever had began this way.

My father had lived in Te Kūiti his whole life. So had his parents. He was born there and now his name was on a sign outside an accountancy firm. He seemed to be always on his way to and from the office in his blue Fiat Tipo, his only passengers the many lever-arch files sliding around in the backseat. Or he was off to rehearsals for the town plays he acted in. He lived deeply inside the town, was known to everybody; perhaps because of this, he seemed to live elsewhere from me. As I got older, we had less and less to say to each other. By the time I was ten we had stopped speaking to each other much at all. I avoided him and he seemed to avoid me too. I watched as he made people laugh on the stage, his hair talcum-powdered gray, playing various comically unhinged old men: a vicar, a murderer, a hapless husband.

He also had a forensic knowledge of Te Kūiti, and this made him even more difficult for me to understand. Why would you bother learning about this place? There was nothing here. But he knew the town from all directions, because as well as being an accountant he was a pilot. From the backseat of his four-seater Cherokee, squashed between my mother and one of my brothers, I would watch him at the controls. And despite myself, when I studied the back of his head, the fat headphones cushioning his ears and a microphone under his chin, a profound trust rose in me. He knew where he was going and exactly how to get there, whether we were going as far as Oamaru, where my grandparents lived, or to Kinloch or Raglan, where we would swim. He knew how to fly through storms that threw us sideways, through blanketing fog and bulleting rains. He knew how to do aerobatics—loops, spins, rolls, vertical lines—though I'd only ever seen this from the ground, looking up with horror, wondering if he was shouting swear words inside the cockpit. My trust of his knowledge felt uncomfortably like love.

My father knew Te Kūiti's history and geography in detail, and when we were all flying together as a family he would point things out to us: rivers, lakes, the houses and farms of people we knew. Watching him maneuver a landing was especially impressive: there was something triumphant in it, and, especially when emerging from a difficult flight, something almost maniacal in his focus. He was like Batman bearing down on a villain in his Batmobile. He'd guide the plane toward the runway, flicking switches and twiddling various knobs, and burbling into a radio. At some point he'd reach a hand up and crank the lever on the ceiling that controlled the plane's nose, the movement a bit like spinning a lasso. The familiar trees and grass stretched up to meet us, and then solid ground was rushing under our wheels. I was always grateful for his calculations and focus at the moment when he returned us to land. There was something magical in how he did it every time. I didn't tell him that, though.

The curious thing was that my father, for all his fixation on money and a sensible career path, had once played music too—had once been in a band, or sort of a band. He would not let us forget this. He had evidence, and his evidence was the Washhouse Tapes. The Washhouse Tapes. The tapes belonged to a better, more hopeful, more creative, more possible time, and as long as we listened to them regularly, that time would never really go away.

The Washhouse Tapes were actually a single, battered cassette tape; the "tapes" referred to the songs on it. Years after the tape was made, then lost, then forgotten, it had been salvaged from a derelict washhouse. Whose washhouse? No one knew. The origins of the songs were even more uncertain. These were songs that my father and his best friend, Hutch, had made when they were teenagers, with their girlfriends—my mother, Julia, and Jenny—mostly on backing vocals. Why did they write those songs? What had they been trying to make happen?

They recorded the songs in the late sixties and early seventies in a cabin at the beach at Mōkau, a West Coast fishing town about one hour's drive from Te Kūiti, with a World War II sea mine mounted on a plinth in the center of the township. At the time of recording, my dad was a young accounting student and ham radio enthusiast, and Hutch was a budding singer-songwriter.

Hutch was the one with the good voice. I thought he sounded a bit like Brian Wilson, his voice full and pure. My father did not have a great singing voice. It was reedy and tuneless and also held a strange urgency, which seemed to exacerbate the reediness. While Hutch sang tunefully and played guitar, banjo, piano, or accordion, Dad would just roar, while bashing on a beer crate, slapping his thighs, hitting a coal scuttle with a stick, or making beeping noises on his ham radio set. In the recordings, he sounds like a kid still discovering the magic of recording sounds and being able to play them back to himself. He reminds me of the actor he became as an adult—unleashed from himself, somehow.

The music, recorded by bouncing tracks between tape recorders so as to build up layers of sound, carried echoes of their favorite music at the time: Bob Dylan, the Beach Boys, the Beatles. You could hear it in the harmonies, the chord changes. At the same time, the songs were of small-town New Zealand, full of references to places like Ruatoria, Mōkau, Ōtāhuhu, Porirua, Hangatiki. But then, every so often, they would wander elsewhere. "Went on down to Santa Fe," Hutch crooned, or "I'm just a punk . . . at Punk Junction." Wherever that was.

Many of the songs on those old Washhouse Tapes were meant to be absurd. You could tell this by their titles: "Meals on Wheels on Fire," "Deaf Monkey," "Waiting for My Eggs to Come," "Amazing Grapes," "Yodeling Night Cart Man." In "Let Us Pray," which ridiculed the church services they'd endured as kids, and which they still felt compelled to attend, Dad shouted "LET US PRAY" over and over at the top of his lungs, like a minister who'd finally lost it at his congregation, until the song sputtered out. Other songs just broke up into discordant noise, as if all the instruments had suddenly disintegrated. But there were one or two songs that were quieter, almost tender, like one called "Gartho," sung by Hutch's girlfriend, Jenny, as she played piano. The song was just about missing someone named Gartho, who I thought must have moved away.

When my parents hosted dinner parties, they'd get out the tape and play it. I'd hear the familiar tinny racket, the voices crackling out, the piano with its yellow-sounding keys, and retreat to my room while they sat around crying with laughter. Every so often the battered cassette would be chewed up by a tape deck, and the tangled magnetic spools would have to be teased out and rewound. Hutch and Jenny's daughters hated the Washhouse Tapes even more than I did, and protested vehemently, cruelly, whenever one of our dads put it on. When their oldest daughter, Jessie, finally shouted, "No one wants to hear your music, Dad," Hutch, now in his fifties with graying ginger hair and aviator spectacles, acquiesced, gently ejecting the tape from the machine.

Te Kūiti, 1964.

The Beatles had conquered England and the States
    worked their magic across the whole world
and finally made their presence felt
down in the heart of the King Country . . .

Backed by a hissing tambourine, these were the opening lines of a song called "The Te Kūiti Underground," which my brother JP, still defiantly playing music, wrote in 2011. The song tells the story of two questing musicians, Garth and Pete, and their attempts to create the "ultimate pop masterpiece" to set alight the musical landscape of provincial New Zealand in the 1960s. After an almost romantic first encounter over the jukebox down at the local pub, transfixed by "I Want to Hold Your Hand," Garth and Pete take a couple of acoustic guitars and a reel-to-reel four-track tape machine out to Mōkau beach. In a cabin "high on a rocky promontory," they record the songs in a creative frenzy—simultaneously working their way through forty-eight cans of beer—while the waves smash down outside. But, of course, the music they make is doomed to obscurity. Perhaps it is too ahead of its time, the men tell each other, and so, with the songs out of their system, they part ways and resign themselves to ordinary lives. Years pass. The cabin at Mōkau is swept away in a storm. And eventually both of the men meet their ends. Garth loses his job and gets drunk one night and falls asleep on the main trunk line. Accidents like these had happened to men and boys in Te Kūiti and in surrounding railway towns; we all knew the stories of traumatized train drivers and the job the police officers had to do the next morning. Pete, meanwhile, dies as an old man, alone and bankrupt. Then, worst of all—"the final nail in the coffin"—is the breakup of the Beatles. When Pete's two sons return to Te Kūiti to clean out their father's flat, they find an old cardboard box in a corner of his garden shed. Inside: the reel-to-reel four-track tape machine; inside that, the tape. At that point, the song breaks out: "Well, the town has changed, and the people have gone, but the Te Kūiti underground lives on—in this song." And then you hear it: a blurt of staticky noise, which I recognize as a few chords of "Deaf Monkey" from the Washhouse Tapes.

It's sentimental. And kind of funny, in its jaunty major key. And perhaps it's an unlikely story—the elements of the Washhouse Tapes story are made so much lonelier, are stretched into myth. But when I heard the song I could almost imagine my parents as young people, apprehensive about their futures. In the Washhouse Tapes, so abrasive in many ways, there was some kind of yearning for other places and other lives. There was also a romanticism of the King Country: this place, for my father and his friends, was as potent as Liverpool in the 1960s. Maybe it was something close to what I'd felt as I walked up the hill, wanting to be away from the house, imagining Paul McCartney at my side: a need to see something more than what was in front of me. It was a yearning I think I sense—in a very small way, hardly registering—even as a kid, when we played the songs on car trips to Mōkau, where we would spend our summers. I couldn't have recognized what it was that I was hearing. But I couldn't imagine not leaving here.

In the early 2000s I'd take the night train from Wellington to Te Kūiti, listening to *The White Album* on my Walkman the whole way, trying to make sense of the passing lights outside. On one occasion, after my mother moved to the South Island for a teaching job, my father came alone to meet me at the station. When I got off the train at three o'clock in the morning, there he was in his railway-station-meeting clothes: a slightly shabby duffel coat—with the hood up, so he had a Grim Reaperish look about him—and big glasses, hands in pockets on the freezing platform.

He brought me back to where he was living, a small and chilly flat with dishes in the sink, towels on the floor, and no pictures on the walls. There was an unfamiliar view of Te Kūiti through the window—you could see across to the other side of the valley, where we had lived before. My parents had sold that house, and my father was getting ready to join my mother on the South Island. He just needed time to wrap up his business.

"It's a major upheaval," I heard him insist more than once, in response to why he was taking so long. "Major upheaval."

After I'd slept a few hours in a fold-out bed in his study, he made us coffee. I watched him carrying out a long-winded filtering method using an old hand grinder and a grease-stained plastic funnel. I recognized that funnel from our garage. I'd used it a few times to funnel milk powder into plastic bottles for newborn lambs. And Dad had used it to funnel oil into the car.

"What is this? What are you doing?"

"What's the problem?" he said. "Gets the job done." And he tried to show me the method he had invented. I shook my head. We drank the coffee silently at the kitchen table. I thought I could taste the old garage.

The filtering method seemed to me a sign of madness. It was

definitely a sign that my dad's world and mine were drifting further apart. I imagined various bits of detritus from our old lives across town becoming strange tools in his solitary life. He would become more and more eccentric in my eyes, and I would become more narrow-minded in his. I thought of him alone in Te Kūiti, in purgatory, never quite ready to carry out the final upheaval. It was easier for me to understand him if I imagined him as a character filled with yearning and loneliness, easier to imagine him meeting his end by falling asleep on the main trunk line than to imagine anything more open-ended and hopeful. One day, I felt sure, my brothers and I would return to this flat and find more of his tapes in a dusty box. Tens of them. And of course the tapes would be filled with songs of yearning, all recorded in my dad's reedy voice.

But finally he did leave the flat. And he did leave the town, and joined my mother in the South Island. He still had the town paper delivered to their new address, and he returned to Te Kūiti often, flying up from the south. He liked to race himself when flying over the Cook Strait, the sea between the two islands, making the crossing as short as possible. Once, he got it down to eighteen minutes.

Flying over a stretch of water feels like moving slowly. Your perception of speed changes because you have no immediate objects by which to judge your speed. But whenever I'm up front in the cockpit with my father, flying north over the water, he accelerates and leans forward somewhat urgently. Below us, on the choppy surface wavelets, darker patches seem to fill the water— the shadows of clouds, like algae blooms. The North Island comes into view, smudged at first, then suddenly hulking, and a few moments later the winds come veering off the hills and hit the plane. Dad grips the controls and bears down.

That morning, after we'd had our coffee and Dad went to work, I walked to the other side of town and up View Road. I'd walked there nearly every day, once, holding Paul's hand and constructing a conversation that served mainly to give Paul opportunities for staring meaningfully at me. There was the smothering gray sky, the fields and gravel roads. Here was the cows' silent evaluation as I walked by. In the distance, the airport. I thought about my boyfriend, a drummer in a band, and how we'd recently held hands in the back of a car, and how thrilling that was. Thinking of it, as I looked up at the huge pine trees that moved slowly in the wind, my excitement made me almost physically sick. I tried to imagine him walking next to me. We'd share an uncomfortable but exciting silence, pausing to point out landmarks below us, including his parents' farm and the long driveway that ran to it. I found I couldn't picture his face as vividly as I would like, couldn't call up his exact expressions and mannerisms at will, though we'd met several times. He kept slipping out of my grasp, as if the road couldn't contain anything real about him. At one point I imagined him jumping a fence and sprinting silently down a hill away from me. I kept walking to the top of the road. Even the sewage pond looked pretty from here, shining silver. I turned around and walked down.

postie

> As the son of a peasant, I want to live and die so
> as to prove that there are also men of genius and
> of energy in my station.
> —*Ferdinand Cheval*

He was walking through Hauterives valley on his postal route when he stumbled and almost fell over. When he collected himself, he saw a strangely shaped rock on the path. He picked it up and studied it, and found it beautiful. The valley of Hauterives is alluvial, filled with stones smoothed by water; the stone in his hand was like a white ball. He wrapped it in a handkerchief and put it in his pocket to look at more closely later.

Ferdinand Cheval had been a postal worker for eight years.

His mail route snaked for more than thirty kilometers through rocky fields toward the town of Hauterives, in Drôme, south-eastern France. He sometimes slept in a barn along the way. I see him in a corner, curled like a length of rope, sleeping with the mice and the rats. Then he'd wake alone and keep going.

The day after he stumbled on the strange rock, he went back to the same place. There were other rocks there that seemed even more beautiful than the rock he had picked up the day before. Each seemed to him an intricate work of sculpture. It must have been around this time—these early days of stumbling, of marveling—that he had his idea.

Once free of his letters, he would pick up stones from the road and carry them in his trouser pockets. When his pockets grew holey, he used a basket that he carried on his back, and then a wheelbarrow. The wheelbarrow became his companion, his "faithful mate of misery." As a cartoon, he would be a thin, coated figure with a black hat, a chevron moustache and a knotted scarf, squashed brown shoes, legs like violin bows. You always see him walking, never riding a horse or a bicycle; always walking, even in the rain, especially in the rain.

There was a period in his life, back before he took a pledge to become a postman, when he left Hauterives to find work and just disappeared. No one knew where he was, not even Rosalie Revol, the young woman he married before he left. There is no record of him for six years. When he returned to Hauterives in 1863, still a young man, Rosalie was waiting for him. She gave birth to their first son, Victorin, the following year, but the boy lived only a year. They had another son, Ferdinand Cyril, soon after. And in 1873, when Cheval had been working as a postman for some time, Rosalie, too, died. Ferdinand couldn't take care of his son on his own. He asked his godparents to take care of his son, and he went on with delivering the mail. Despite his constant work, Cheval found a second wife, Marie-Philomène Richaud. With her he had a daughter, Alice-Marie-Philomène, who died suddenly at fifteen. We read that Cheval was overwhelmed by this loss.

Progress was slow. He worked during the day, and worked more at night with an oil lamp. Some days, it seemed there was less of the work, that it wasn't evolving at all but devolving. It crumbled upward and downward; windows broke open, then shut; figures and trees emerged, then seemed to hunch down and recede into the stones.

It is difficult to find accounts of Cheval's day-to-day life. Most accounts frame his story in the vague terms of the inexorable march of his work—his determination to create his vision at all costs. I can only imagine that he was lonely out there, that as he grew older his walk became stilted, his bending for stones more occasional. Still he continued. When he wasn't walking and bending, he must have been building: piling stone upon stone upon stone. Every stone he thought more beautiful than the last, and his excitement at such beauty just lying there at his feet—not to mention his conviction that he was creating something extraordinary—propelled him forward.

The shapes were becoming representations of real things. He was making the Taj Mahal of Agra in India, the Maison Carrée de Nîmes in southern France, a medieval castle, a mosque. Maybe these were places he had seen on the postcards he delivered. Among the structures were animals: bears, elephants, sheepdogs, ostriches, flamingos, eagles, geese. His building was a fusion of references to plant, animal, and human worlds, and to his own fantasies. The building was not and would not be beautiful, but in the end it might look as though it once had been.

Thirty-three years after he stumbled on that stone on his postal route, Cheval was in his seventies, withered and triumphant, and the building was complete. He inscribed whimsical maxims into the stones he had once carried in his pockets. And he made a small altar for his wheelbarrow, the same one he'd had for decades. "I finally found what I was looking for, digging . . . to shape out of the earth this fairy palace. For my ideals, my body suffered, braving the weather, criticisms and years." He called his building Palais Idéal, although in his letter to an archivist he said that at first he'd hoped for it to be called Seul au Monde, Alone in the World.

He had also hoped to be buried inside his palace. When the authorities declined permission, he built himself a tomb from stones, which took him another eight years. He named it the Tomb of Silence and Endless Rest.

He was an old man when he died, his body frayed from walking, his knees—as they say of the knees of old men—gnarled as the roots of trees. His palace and tomb became a destination for tourists. In photographs of the site, visitors wander around with cameras, and before them the palace looks inhospitable: the body of a huge, hibernating animal.

The building itself resists categorization. It tries to be everything and everywhere. To Cheval it was simply "this wonderful work," something to be marveled at. In some ways what Cheval thought about his work suggests one way of thinking about his life. Both seem to hold a simple message: how wonderful it is if we just keep going—and how wonderful it is that a simple stumbling block can set us on the path of our life's work, can change the entire story of our lives and deaths. His story has been fashioned as a beacon for others, especially for the plodders among us: he not only achieved something extraordinary, but did so as a simple postman who ignored the mocking of his neighbors. His own writings have fed into this story. "1879–1912," he inscribed under a stairway of his palace, "10,000 days, 93,000 hours, 33 years of obstacles and trials. The work of one single man."

Still, like some kind of invisible scaffold, solitude and grief and even misery press upon that work. These things are surely as present in any life as the need to make something extraordinary, but the famous story of Cheval dictates that his need eclipse all else in his life. Perhaps he truly did want everyone to see the palace looming in the distance and be drawn to it. Perhaps he wanted only for people to crawl up inside it, like bats, so they could see how intricate and colossal his achievement was; that out of solitude, out of the accusations of madness, can come something that rises. We can't know, now. The palace teems with his ideas about people and places, as if he were looking to make a version of the world that he could truly inhabit and understand. In that way it seems a monument to loneliness. And his pride seems a testament to needing almost nothing from the world—only the stones next to his feet. In the valley, the palace juts at the skyline, weird and knobbly and forever breaking apart.

on any walk

On any walk into dense bush, at some point we ask one another, "Why are we doing this?" We could be at home, we say, where there is hot water and a flushing toilet. The question ripples up and down the chain of walkers, and one or two people raise the serious possibility of turning back right now. Their voices are bright with certainty, seeming almost to hold apart the foliage we are struggling through, making our way easier for a moment. Surely we'll stop walking, stand there befuddled as if shaking ourselves out of a dream, and then one by one we'll turn around, shaking our heads and laughing, and the person bringing up the rear will turn into the leader. But even as the dissenters are saying the words—"I really think we should turn back!"—we all, together, remember how far we have come and how much distance would be wasted if we were to turn back. The day would be rendered pointless. We should at least dignify how far we have come by going a bit further.

As we turn a corner, we hear the roar of a river. The roar seems to come from somewhere low, under the trees, seething in the ground. We are reassured that our destination, the river, lies just ahead. The path is beginning to fade in and out, becoming threadbare as we continue. As we push thorny branches out of the way, sometimes they accidentally ricochet into the face of the person following. No one is enjoying the walk. Has anyone ever enjoyed the walk? Perhaps none of us ever enjoyed it, even early on when our legs were fresh. Maybe even back then we all secretly wished it were over. Even as we agree that the pieces of sky through the trees are very blue, as we admire the persistence of the tiny streams, the marvel of the koura scrambling through them, a thought hums between us: If we had turned back before, we would be home now. We try to recall some sweeter hours when we weren't thinking about the end, but our memory is blurred by footsteps and by the sticky wash of leaves against bodies.

The river roars, or seems to roar. A small voice asks if maybe we should stop and rest for a few minutes. Not turn back, understand; just rest. There is a momentary slackening of pace, and uncertainty ripples up and down our number. But then a sharper voice responds that if we did stop to rest, even for a few minutes, we would still be thinking about walking, calculating the distance that remained, which is a kind of walking in itself, only a motionless internal one, like the spinning beach ball on a computer—so it wouldn't be true rest. It would be a false rest. This is a persuasive argument and we all agree immediately to continue on, and our pace gathers again. There is, at least, solidarity in the walking, a feeling of being a part of things. We keep our eyes on the back of the person in front of us, whose leg hairs are aquiver with burrs. Our ears strain for the river. We will reach the river sooner now that we have not stopped.

From time to time, we imagine ourselves in a clearing, sitting on our humped packs in the shade—past selves who stopped to rest back there. A small crowd of them are sitting in the prickling grass. They are no longer a forward-facing line but a stagnant scattering, doing nothing but taking in air. They are utterly still, as if they will never move and never be found again, as if they are items accidentally dropped from a pocket, falling farther and farther behind us now.

big red

and surely we shall not continue to be unhappy
we shall be happy
but we shall continue to be ourselves everything
                              continues to be possible
—Frank O'Hara, "Adieu to Norman,
Bon Jour to Joan and Jean-Paul"

At the library I waited on the landing by the café. Below the railing, on the ground floor, there were gray coats, black coats, brown coats. And then a block of red: JP striding through the automatic doors, his jacket swinging open as he bounded up the steps two at a time.

"Eyelash! Sorry I'm late. I was besieged by slow walkers."

A few people were already looking in our direction—my brother's voice is loud and expressive, and his name for me, Eyelash, always sounds odd in public. My brother looked a bit odd, too, in his oversized red NZ Post jacket and shorts and Post-issued socks, which he wore mid-ankle so that the envelope icons could be seen clearly. His legs were like a caricature of good legs: tanned, hairy, with tough, balled calves. "Sorry about the uniform. It's to the discredit of the postal service that these uniforms don't blend seamlessly in cafés."

I'd asked JP to meet me that day because I wanted to tell him I was thinking of writing about the underground music scene in Hamilton in the late 1990s. About the bands of that time, bands that sparked brightly and then vanished, bands like JP's own, the Clampers. I had vague but great ambitions for this piece, though I doubted I would ever publish it—it probably wouldn't make sense to anyone beyond our family—but that didn't particularly matter to me. It would be about the edges of music, the edges of Hamilton, the underbelly of our town. It would be about drunkenness to keep warm in winter, about cars stuffed with guitars, drum kits stuffed with pillows. It would incorporate loosely connected anecdotes that were essentially insignificant but that I thought were funny, like the time we saw the band Mercury Rev play in Auckland City—two and a half hours' drive from our town—and our mother couldn't get a ticket, but afterward said she'd actually been able to hear the music faintly from the car in the parking lot and had had a very nice time. My enthusiasm for the story was such that I felt it would write itself. All I needed to do was grab hold of one end and pull the rest up behind it, like electrical wire out of the ground.

"Don't worry," I told JP. "I'll change anything incriminating."

I told JP that I wanted Big Red to be in the piece too, some-how, even in passing, a ghost in the night. I wanted to cast it as a kind of symbol—of what, I wasn't sure yet—or even a character in its own right.

To my relief, JP seemed pleased about my idea. "Big Red, resurrected!"

In the children's section below where we sat, a boy had up-ended a whole row of books from a shelf. He sat on the floor surrounded by books and howled.

We turned back to our coffee. "What happened to Big Red, anyway?" I said.

And that would be one of the last times I would see JP just as he was: my brother, unwritten.

I'd thought he had found the jacket in a linen cupboard at home in Te Kūiti. It was in a polythene sack full of winter clothes that one of my mother's well-meaning friends had given to us. Among the thicket of bush socks, duffel coat as black as a dog, and sticky woolen jumpers, there was the jacket, ready to be hoisted like a flag.

In fact, the jacket had once belonged to one of my mother's colleagues at the local high school, a popular but terrifying English teacher with stony blue eyes and white-blond hair that stood on end and that he often ran his hands through in exasperation. He threw chairs against the wall and sometimes taught his classes standing on his desk like Mr. Keating from *Dead Poets Society*. I remember his red socks. I adored him. So did my mother; they were firm friends. He left our family with some of the things he wasn't able to take with him when he moved away to London—boxes full of Kinks and Split Enz and Police records, music biographies, and some clothes, including the jacket.

The jacket was soft and puffy, with a gathered waist and a high collar with odd tan stripes on it. It was essentially a bomber jacket. It had snap buttons down the front. Its flight-silk sleeves were full and shiny, but the cuffs were snugly elasticated. A stunt pilot from Reno might have stepped from his plane wearing such a jacket. It was a true red—a Postman Pat red, an American-sunset red, almost the red of the saveloy sausages our grandmother ladled onto our plates in Oamaru. And it was warm, which was important, because that winter JP was living in a room underneath a house on Memorial Drive in Hamilton, and it was always cold there. His room had louvered windows and a puddle under the door. It was a bit like living inside a log.

He started wearing the jacket everywhere. He wore it when he walked across the overhead bridge to the polytechnic where he was doing his songwriting degree. It billowed out behind him like an extra body. He wore it into the CD store where the girl he liked worked. When he came home to Te Kūiti on weekends, I was briefly enveloped in the jacket, and again before he left. "Take it easy, Eyelash," he said, and I watched him bump down Sturgess Terrace in the family Ford Cortina, in which Dad had helped him get his driver's license.

The jacket was the first thing he put on each morning. He pulled it right over the green, polka-dotted, knee-length smock from Postie Plus that he slept in. I picture him running barefoot from his room under the house, up the lawn, and into the kitchen at Mem Drive, as everyone called the huge old building. Mem

Drive housed many transients, but besides JP there was another mainstay, an artist called Snakes.

Snakes was from London. "His work is quite famous in some countries," JP once told me, "but no one really knows who he is in New Zealand." I never knew Snakes's original name, but he had changed it by deed poll to Emit Snake-Beings, which JP pronounced "Ee-mit Snake Beans." He'd worked as a prop maker and lighting technician on movie sets, and had founded a garden company. He now spent a lot of his time at the kitchen table or in a loft up in the ceiling, which was his bedroom and also his workshop. His artworks or "shrines," mounted in glass cases on walls around the house, were constructed from electrical odds and ends: live and dead lightbulbs, sparkplugs, telephone receivers, electric fans, grandfather clock faces. Some were coin-operated; you could make the lights flash and flicker and the wheels spin. Or other things would happen: a tape would play street sounds from countries around the world, or electric fans would blast cold air onto your hands.

The shrines all had grand names: "Shrine to the Dead Light Bulb." "Shrine to the Alchemical Essence of Time." "Basilica of the Tattooist." "Mechanical Divination and Prayer Machine." "Random Divinity Selector." There was something anatomical about the shrines. In their glass cases they bristled with potential energy. They frightened me slightly in the same way Gene Wilder as Willy Wonka frightened me, with his glassy smile and non sequiturs meant to charm you but that hinted at some underlying menace.

Mem Drive itself felt like an abandoned playground. Inside it were childhood things that had faded and warped. Wherever you turned there was something to startle you: a clump of grinning sock monkeys, a painting of horses and elephants up high on bony legs like stilts, a trapdoor in the pantry that might admit a stranger in the night. The high, cracked ceilings made the house enormous. It dwarfed everyone who lived there—everyone, it seemed to me, but Snakes. He was its heart.

One morning, when JP burst into the kitchen in his red jacket, Snakes looked up from his breakfast and announced, "Hey, it's JP and big red!" And because JP respected Snakes, the jacket became Big Red. Naming it gave it permanence, like naming a car. At Mem Drive, with its trapdoors and shrines, Big Red fit in perfectly.

No matter its history, though, or how warm it was, or who might once have worn it, Big Red was ugly. That's all it was, and, I thought, all it could ever be. Neither fashion nor irony had circled back far enough to reach that jacket. I could not imagine a time when wearing something so terrible would mean that you were pointing and laughing at fashion's fickleness and that this awareness meant that you looked cool. When JP bounded into Mem Drive's kitchen with a guitar case under one arm and the jacket zipped under his chin, our older brother, Neil, looked injured. "JP. You're not wearing that out, are you?"

JP hitched his legs apart like a cowboy and narrowed his eyes. "You got a problem with Big Red?" he asked. In moments of tension, he always adopted an American accent. We all did. It seemed to lighten the mood, in the same way that turning on the radio made silence more bearable.

"Damn right," Neil drawled. "That's the most godawful goddamn jacket anybody's ever seen. I won't be seen with it." The accent faded and we saw that he was serious.

It was the oldest scene I knew: my brothers starting out joking and ending up fighting. This time, though, it wasn't over a computer game or a packet of biscuits—this was fashion, something you weren't supposed to care about, and there were no rules, except that anything you said would, without fail, be proven wrong. Neil was now a serious university scholar, but he rarely won these arguments. As he tried to get through to JP, his voice would waver and crack, and he'd burst into outraged laughter. During these arguments he and JP spoke in different languages, moved at different speeds, stood at opposite sides of the room shouting at each other. They looked as huge and battle-hungry as Achilles and Hector from my Reader's Digest *Myths and Legends* encyclopedia.

"Hey!" JP countered, holding up his knobby hands. "Fine by me, brother! Nobody else cares about my jacket. They'll all be looking at you, anyway." Neil snorted. He was good-looking and hated people to think that he knew it, but he was far too good-looking not to know. JP knew this. When the university used Neil's picture in posters advertising its master of arts program, and the posters were stolen all over the campus, we all knew why.

We were on our way to the JBC, a live music venue in the basement of a building formerly used as a pool hall. The abbreviation stood for "Jazz Blues Concept," but I never saw any jazz or blues there—only rock bands. You could sit on couches and deep armchairs to watch bands playing on the low plinth up at the front. The JBC felt like a sanctuary from the rest of Hamilton: a cavern full of people cheering one another on. The bar was maybe the length of a car's bumper and the carpet was dark orange. This night JP had a gig there with the Clampers; I was only fifteen, but JP and Neil were going to smuggle me in. "We'll say you're my girlfriend or something," Neil said. The plan was a flawed one—we were unmistakably related, and I was unmistakably not eighteen—but I agreed and tried not to think about it.

Instead, I thought about my outfit. I was wearing brown flares and a blue-and-pink-flowered shirt from the Hamilton Salvation Army. I felt good. Fashion from the seventies was reckless and daring, but also clever, and I believed that these qualities were somehow transferred to me when I wore the clothes. Before we set off for the JBC, I studied myself long and hard in my bedroom mirror. I put on some lipstick and rubbed it off with a tissue so that only a stain was left, then combed back my eyelashes with one of my mother's hair curlers. "Yes," I whispered, and smiled at myself. For a long time I practiced that smile, waiting for it to seem spontaneous and charming. My teeth were small and frilled at the edges. There was a strawberry blotch of eczema at one corner of my mouth. I poked at it for a long time with a stick of concealer.

Neil, as usual, looked terrific in his blue denim jacket and green T-shirt with *Yes* printed diagonally on it. His hair was artfully mussed.

As we were heading out, he tried one more time. "Look, JP, I've got a jacket you can borrow." Plaintively, and seemingly out of nowhere, he held up a garment that looked like a piece of corrugated iron.

JP grunted. "Nah! I've got Big Red."

We got into Neil's car and rode in silence while I stole glances at the rearview mirror, trying to catch myself looking eighteen.

Just as JP was abandoning fashion, Neil and I had been finding it, and fashion equipped us with new ways of being embarrassed. There were so many more ways to be unfashionable than fashionable, and the distinction was always so slight: a glimpse of white socks, an overly tight waistband, sweatshirt cuffs riding high on bony arms. JP knew them all, the unfashionable ways. He wore his track pants hitched high and a brown cardigan buttoned from top to bottom. He wore an old suit jacket with a T-shirt and cargo shorts, and socks balled around his ankles. He carried things *inside* the pockets of the cargo shorts, even though those pockets, we all knew, were not meant for cargo.

If there was one garment that gathered up all of these qualities like a black hole, it was Big Red. "If people are worth my time, they won't care!" he reasoned. He told us that Big Red was a test—a test of people's substance, of their ability to look beyond surface, and ultimately of their strength of character.

"Big Red isn't the sum of my parts. He's just the beginning," JP insisted, as if the philosophy behind the jacket was so strong that it should eclipse the sight of the jacket itself. The deeper part of me tried hard to believe this, and understood that somewhere in JP's reasoning there was truth. The rest of me knew that these arguments meant nothing to the faces on a street. I feared those faces. They would never see further than the beginning. In Hamilton, that was all you were. But JP was fearless.

Big Red was the apotheosis of everything that I knew to be different about my brother: his bounding walk; the way he said "Yeah!" repeatedly, with vigorous nodding; his excruciating politeness; his labored enunciation. Sometimes he gave words their own special twist. The word *writhing* he pronounced "wreething" and the word *fug* he pronounced "fugue." Perhaps, when he said his head was in a fug, he meant just what he said—that his head was surrounded by a cloud of tubas and trumpets. Or maybe it was the other kind of fugue, the one where suddenly, out of the blue, you don't know who you are. I registered these differences only with embarrassment. Because I was someone who was always trying to change certain things about myself, I felt only the frustration of not being able to change certain things about my brother.

"Are you from South Africa?" people asked when they heard JP speak.

"No." None of us had ever been to South Africa. "I'm actually from Te Kūiti." His father had lived in Te Kūiti all his life, he explained, as if this were the key to the mystery.

I got into the JBC on account of being with the band. JP and his guitar case brought an air of officialdom to all of us, and the man at the door pressed a stamp to my wrist without even glancing at my carefully made-up face. I followed JP and Neil tentatively. JP took off the jacket before joining the other band members—Geordie, Samuel, Struan—who were setting up.

As always, when the stage lights went up and JP started to sing, I was surprised. Where had that voice come from? "You know," Neil said, as if it were just between the two of us, "JP has an excellent voice." We'd heard him many times, of course—but hearing it on stage made it more significant. Doing something well in public made it real; having other people see it made it even realer. It was a bit like a local band like Crowded House making it big in America: only then could the band be celebrated in New Zealand. Hearing JP perform in public made us pay attention. His voice was difficult to describe. It was sort of cavernous, upward moving. It was also very slightly, harmlessly out of tune. Like the needle on a seismometer, it wobbled slightly around the level line, never quite coming to rest. When layered on a four-track, it made a sweet and ghostly choir.

At the same time, hearing him sing was slightly embarrassing. Singing fell into the category of self-expression, and none of us was openly expressive at home, unless it was obviously a joke or an imitation of someone else, like my father doing an impression of the local radio DJ or one of the other pilots out at the aero club. Whenever I wanted to sing or dance, I would wait until no one was home, or barricade the door to the living room, before letting loose. But neither of these methods guaranteed privacy: one of my brothers would come home early and burst through the door just when I was starting my howling routine at the piano, or—worse—my mother would wander in mid-chorus and say brightly, "That's lovely, Ashleigh!" Even when I successfully barricaded the door, my family would still find ways to defeat my efforts. Neil once climbed in through the window and hid behind the curtains, until his loud snickering at my dance-floor convulsions to Tom Petty and the Heartbreakers gave him away.

In Hamilton, the Clampers song "Wish You Was Mine" had been played on the student radio station, which, in my mind, meant that it was famous. It had also been included on a Hamilton compilation called *Year Zero*—and it was the last track on that compilation, a position of honor, because people always want something to remember at the end.

> *I wish you was mine*
> *until the dust on your shoes becomes ice*
> *and the blood in your veins becomes wax*
> *and the wind and rain say—hey*
> *wish you was mine*

A curious thing to do was to watch girls as they watched JP sing. I noticed that they went quiet and still. They didn't stare, exactly—all girls seemed to approach my brother with a sort of caution—they just measured him up, perhaps trying to measure his blond hair and handsome face against his unusual manner. When he sang, his eyes went wide and he stared intently into the middle distance, as if singing to someone nobody else could see. He grimaced and did falsetto shrieks. The Hamilton crowd cheered as if he were their star, an anti-star.

After the gig, though, as the band clumped off the stage and toward the bar, JP put on Big Red, and in an instant everything changed. His arms and chest ballooned. His face appeared to mottle. He was a stunt pilot with no aircraft. The balance between strangeness and charm tipped sharply back to strange—and I felt a sharp and selfish disappointment. It was Big Red's fault. Now JP was someone those same girls would pretend they didn't know if they saw him walking toward them, someone their boyfriends might yell at out the window as they drove past in their souped-up cars. Hamilton always let you know when you were drawing too much attention to yourself.

As we sat in the library trying to unpick those days, I asked JP what had happened to Big Red. He thought about it for a while.

"We were about to go to the Waitomo pub, I think. Neil and those guys wanted to give me a makeover." He shook his head. "It was a ridiculous scene." He often referred to incidents in this way—a "bad scene," a "diabolical scene," somebody had been "lurching drunkenly around the scene"—as if anything that might happen was pre-scripted, and all JP could do was stumble into it, improvising his lines.

They were sitting around a table, drinking, eating, shouting. Stereo speakers were roaring—probably Nirvana or the Smashing Pumpkins or the Stone Temple Pilots—and beer cans were all over the table. My brothers were with two close friends of Neil's: Stables, a soft-spoken drummer on whom I'd long nursed a painful crush, and Tutty, a singer and brilliant pianist. The three of them—Neil, Stables, and Tutty—had formed a band they'd called Spaz.

At one point, Tutty announced that it was cold and they should build a fire. "I'm gonna go chop some wood," he said, and then he eyed JP, snug in his jacket. By this point Big Red was starting to leak stuffing from its cuffs and take on the slight but unmistakable smell of mildew. "Can I borrow that? It's cold outside."

"Why don't you wear your own jacket?"

Tutty stared at him for a moment. Then he pounced and wrestled JP to the ground amidst the guitar leads and pedals. He pulled the jacket off JP, stood up, put his arms into the sleeves— it was far too small for his large lanky frame—and then he disappeared through the kitchen door, leaving JP bemused on the carpet.

When Tutty returned a while later with the firewood, he was still wearing his thick woolen farm jumper, but no jacket.

JP demanded, "Where's Big Red?"

Tutty was tall, and his algae-green mohawk made him taller. Even when the mohawk lay flat and eel-like on his scalp, it made me nervous; it was like someone carrying a knife. Tutty had wild blue eyes and hands big enough to span well over an octave on the piano; his scream, when he fronted Spaz, gave me goosebumps. He had once played and sung all of "Stairway to Heaven" on the grand piano at the Te Kūiti Civic Centre in front of hundreds of people, most of them elderly and, I suspected, unfamiliar with Led Zeppelin. That night I had performed too, playing a piece called "The Sea Is Angry" by William Alwyn, which was full of severe volume contrasts and menacing arpeggio. I'd played it badly: too quickly, with a liberal scattering of bung notes, and without sufficient anger. As I sidled red-faced back into the audience, my piano teacher, Mrs. Archibald, gave me a single grave nod. I longed for the gumption, the hands, the talent of Tutty.

In the kitchen, Tutty took a long swig from his beer. He wiped the back of his hand across his mouth and said, "Fuck Big Red."

No one knows what happened. I imagined it, though. I imagined it like the climax of a horror film.

I saw the jacket arcing through the air with arms out wide, going up like a flame through the trees. I saw it curled in one corner of the field, moldering to gray, then sinking slowly into the mud, the way dead sheep do. I saw Tutty spreading Big Red across the chopping block, and in the grimy half-light out there, picking up an axe, the short-handled one with the orange head rusted brown. I saw his giant fingers curled around the handle. His breath, a rush of white that pixelates in the air.

"I knew something bad had happened," JP told me. "I went out to the garden, but there was nothing there." That night, as he squinted up at Tutty, I think he knew he wouldn't see Big Red again.

There's no way of knowing. You sometimes saw a lost piece of clothing at the adventure playground at school, usually a navy blue jumper, the unofficial school uniform. Did the owner know it was lost? Were they coming back for it? Or would it be delivered by the caretaker to the lost property box, dampened with dew and rain and scratchy with debris?

It was true that I didn't care for Big Red. But I didn't like the fact that nobody would come back for it. Nobody would deliver it to a place of rest, a place of official lostness from which it might be recovered. It was out there somewhere but was also gone forever.

After being given more to drink, JP was finally made over: black trousers, gelled hair, and a long gray jacket. "You look fucking cool," cried Tutty. "You're gonna get laid tonight."

Years later, JP laughed it off. "Maybe it was time to move on," he said to me. "Every time I wore Big Red, I felt like I was going into battle. Explaining myself to everyone." He shrugged and said in an American accent, "A man gets tired."

The jacket was replaced by a series of op-shop cardigans—brown, green, navy—in which JP, with his long arms and bony wrists, looked somehow malnourished. He wore the cardigans with baggy cord pants (to which he paid tribute in a song: "In the bottomless pockets of my green-brown cords / who knows what I'll find?") and scuffed school shoes. His wardrobe was also shaped by Neil, who donated his old clothes to JP: a denim jacket, the green *Yes* T-shirt, and various woolly jumpers, all of which JP wore until they were unrecognizable as things Neil had once worn. At first it was odd to see JP without Big Red, as if his body itself had changed shape. I'd got used to the slow disintegration of the jacket. I had believed I would see it to the end, right down to the bloodshot threads. Years later I borrowed the *Yes* T-shirt and never returned it, wearing it under my own cardigans until it was as thin as a greenish shadow on my skin.

JP left school not sure what he would do. A career advisor had suggested he might make a good journalist, so after dithering for a while, he enrolled in a journalism course. He dropped out after a year, enrolled in music studies at the polytechnic, and switched to songwriting, which he was good at. But during the holidays he had to work. "You've gotta have money coming in," said Dad.

JP pruned trees on a hill, getting paid tree by thorny tree, but he worked so slowly that he made well below minimum wage, at that time about six dollars per hour. He worked as a kitchen hand at a café in Waitomo alongside our mother. But perhaps because of the low-level tinnitus he'd developed from playing in the Clampers, he struggled to make out the high-octane questions and commands over the clanking of cutlery and whirring of microwaves, and eventually he was let go. Then came Omya, the limeworks, which meant shoveling lime, sweeping lime, bagging lime, and crawling through a narrow tunnel to heave lime rocks into wheelbarrows. He cleaned Hamilton office buildings for a man who would hover nearby with hands on hips, critiquing his vacuuming. One summer he went to Cairns in Australia to pick mangoes, and developed a full-body skin rash from the hundred-degree heat and the caustic sap of the hundreds of mangoes he lifted down from the trees with a picking stick.

For a while he worked as a mushroom picker, crouching for hours in a half-lit, subterranean room. "They're unnaturally pale," he said of his coworkers, "like mushrooms, in fact. Most of them seem quite insane." But he sounded philosophical. He told me about his coworkers. Some had worked in factories like this for their whole lives. Some had endured terrible things. JP could always get people to talk about themselves and to tell him their stories.

It was on the way back to Hamilton, after picking mushrooms one night, that his job ended suddenly. The air was full of mist. The Cortina was a demanding car, requiring vigorous wrenching of the column gearshift and pumping of the clutch. JP was about ten minutes from home.

The back road leading into Te Kūiti from the north, Hangatiki East Road, has gently rolling, marshy fields on either side. There are a few cowsheds, and a few far-apart houses with trees grown around them. I imagine that JP wound down the window to let the night come in. Maybe he was relieved to feel the cool air on his face and arms after the sterile fug of the mushroom-growing facility. He was a considerate driver who always dipped his headlights to oncoming cars, and this night he decided to keep them fully dipped because it wasn't easy to see through the mist anyway.

He was moving fast enough that when a heavy object smashed into the car it threw him forward, then whipped him back. Instinctively he braked—I imagine he was yelling, although for some reason I still picture this scene unfolding in silence—but not in time to avoid another crash. It wasn't the crashing of metal and glass; it was a heavy, hard thud, like being struck with a giant mallet. In a Cortina, every jolt is amplified—it's a brittle, sensitive car, sitting high on the road, as if to attention—and the collision reverberated through the car in waves. Then the motor cut out and everything went very still. All around was a howling, baying sound.

"I got out," he told me later. "I thought I might be having a dream."

I picture him standing alone on the road, panting, the motor coughing, and two cows lying on their sides on the cold road. The noise fills his ears, and fills his head, blood, and lungs. By now the night has gone completely black, as if a heavy bowl has been set down around him. The rest of this scene has been drawn with a charcoal stick. There's a shiny black road, deep black hills, bright blips of faraway houses. JP's face is white and his eyes are black holes. The moon has been penciled in and then rubbed out.

He left the cows and the car. He ran until he found a house with a porch light on. His footsteps made no sound, as if the crash had shaken all the weight out of his body. The farmer inside the house accompanied him back to the road with a gun. The farmer shot the cow that hadn't already died, while JP sat miserably on the road's edge. The two animal bodies were huge in the darkness. Nearby, the Cortina hissed and ticked.

I think I remember afterward. Neil, my parents, and I are assembled in our pajamas in the kitchen. My father is inconsolable. "I don't believe it," he keeps saying, his voice pinched with rage. "I don't believe it." Meanwhile, JP receded into his cardigan. "It wasn't really my fault, Dad," he says blearily. "Someone left a gate open."

Logic tells me this kitchen scene can't have happened. JP was in Hamilton: he must have phoned from Mem Drive to tell one of my parents about the cows. Maybe my memory is superimposing one thing on another: the sound of my father exclaiming into the hallway telephone, and a different pajama-clad kitchen assembly. The sound of my father's voice when enraged is easy to call up, perhaps because it was so rare for him to raise his voice. There was the time he backed his car into a wheelbarrow left in the driveway—*That's a thousand bucks of damage!*—or the time his whole body convulsed with fright, his feet ejecting from the floor, as JP and I burst out from behind a door to surprise him when he arrived home from work: *Don't DO that!* Such scenes leap at me and collide in midair.

JP had always been restless at night. As an eight- or nine-year-old he would hurry around the house after dark checking the doors, securing them against monsters like the Outsider from Dean Koontz's *Watchers*. Older, he would go for midnight walks with a knife tied around his waist in case he got into trouble. After he ran into the wandering cows, the nightmares sometimes came back.

"The worst thing, if you can say there's a worst thing, was the noise they made," he said. "This keening, crying noise." And then he mimicked the noise. As always, his impression was too good, far too close to the bone.

The destruction of the Cortina had one fortuitous outcome: he no longer had any means of getting to the mushroom farm. And the police exonerated him of all blame.

> *My old man is an astronaut*
> *he built a spaceship on our front lawn.*
> *He made it out of rubber bands*
> *and rusty old baked bean cans.*

This is a song JP composed for the classes he taught during a traveling teaching job. It involved driving (in a new second-hand car, a blue hatchback Toyota) to primary schools around the North Island, starting at Waiōuru, and giving a presentation he called "The Logistics of a Manned Mission to Mars." He made his own cardboard props—Martians, a space shuttle, the nine planets, for there were still nine—and wrote the song "My Old Man," which he played during his presentation.

The presentations were a success: the students thought he was funny. But the job proved exhausting. The driving, the skeptical primary-school teachers, the pressure to entertain with props that were held together with masking tape and pipe cleaners—it sounded fascinating and hilarious when he told people about it, but the job drained him of all energy. He took several months back in Te Kūiti to recuperate, sleeping and thinking and starting to write music again. He was alone with my father in the big house there. When we emailed or talked on the phone I could tell he was unhappy. He was lonely. And there was a kind of shame in going back to Te Kūiti when all your school friends had left. People looked at you a bit too long when you walked down the street. Anytime you went into a shop, you had to have the same conversation: What were you doing back? How long were you staying? "We knew you'd be back," they said.

I was glad when JP decided to leave, finally, and come south to Wellington, where I was. Wellington is a small city but it's still a city; more important, it's a six-hour drive from Te Kūiti, which felt just far enough. By now I had left school one year early to start a bachelor's degree in Wellington. I'd found that I was wildly out of my depth. I sat weeping in the back rows as media studies lecturers spoke alien words at the lectern: *signifier, signified, mythologize*. JP, too, was idly thinking of taking up a degree—maybe in social work, maybe in psychiatry. But first he needed money coming in. He started work as a cleaner at a supermarket, working the night shift; when he wasn't there he was a kitchen hand at the parliament café, Bellamy's, where he served MPs and party leaders. Once he was accidentally elbowed by Prime Minister Helen Clark as she entered the café. My parents were delighted by this story, especially my mother, a fierce Clark supporter. "Imagine! Hustled aside by Helen Clark!"

He started working for the IHC near the end of that year. One of his jobs was to care for a teenage boy with Down syndrome, a sweet-natured seventeen-year-old who called him by his full name, excitedly: "John-Paul Young! John-Paul Young!" Then he met a beautiful woman, a primary-school teacher, who became his girlfriend, the kind of girlfriend who is full of warm laughter, freckles, and strong white teeth; who buys you new clothes and makes sideways references to the future.

Still, when I visited him at his flat on his afternoons off from work, he would appear frowning and rumpled at the door, sometimes in his dressing gown. "Eyelash. Come in." His voice was oddly flat. He was developing Dad's habit of never meeting my eye. He reminded me a little of a fictional character he'd once played in a short film that Neil wrote and directed at university. Neil was an aspiring filmmaker and screenwriter, and JP was always the star of Neil's films—always the superhero or the lab experiment escaping down the hallway. In this film, called *Walter,* JP played a psychically crippled young man who, one day, for whatever reason, decides to eat his pet rat. The film didn't have much of a plot. The rat-eating was really the only event.

For the opening credits, JP was to stand motionless in the kitchen while the Kinks song "Do You Remember Walter?" played behind him. I hung back and watched Neil unfold the tripod. I was nervous, because later I had a pivotal role in the film. I had to run into the kitchen and shout, "Walter, what are you doing?"

As Neil positioned the camera, JP stood there uncertainly. He was wearing Dad's long dressing gown. "What do I do first?" he said.

"Just stand there," Neil instructed. "Just look deranged." He stepped into the frame and placed a vegetable colander on JP's head at a slight tilt, taking a few moments to get it just right, chuckling to himself. Then he stepped back and crouched behind the camera. "Action!"

All at once, JP was Walter. He stared into space with his jaw sagging and his eyes unfocused, his arms heavy at his sides, like a shell-shocked soldier. Bits of blond hair stuck through the holes of the colander. He began to make a faint groaning sound.

Suddenly I was frightened. How readily my brother could make his handsome face fall away to reveal this other terrible face underneath. He had always known what disturbed people. This, I believed, was why he was always the star. Then Neil was shouting. "Hold it. Stop! I forgot to put on the song." JP took off the colander and, to my relief, there he was underneath.

We had our best conversations either walking down a street or driving in his car. The car, the same one he'd taken on his Martian-mission journey, was cluttered with CD cases, bits of clothing, food wrappers, guitar leads, ukuleles. It was like driving around in the wing of one of the stages where he played.

"How's the music going?"

"Ah, it's all right, I guess. I've got a few songs on the boil. I'm thinking of buying a sampler. Or maybe a theremin. They've got a bit of a bad rep, though, theremins. I think horror movies killed them for music. Hannibal Lecter had one, didn't he?"

He was in a new band called Idiomatic. When he performed with them, he was full of energy. He seemed utterly unafraid— of surly bar managers, of falsetto notes, of what anyone thought. On stage, he was fast to retaliate if he thought he'd been slighted, and he could even be prickly. There was an angry quickness that hadn't been there before. "None of you bastards is dancing anyway, so to hell with you all," he told an unresponsive audience. "I'm going to play a ballad."

Idiomatic was full of familiar faces. JP's high school friend Rajesh played electric guitar and sang the occasional backing vocal. His flatmate Penny hammered a drum, sometimes played a kazoo, and sang in a high, sharp voice. A cellist sat to his left, a woman named Jane, who had white-gold hair and who wore corsets and heavy black skirts.

JP's voice was the best, always sweet and resolute.

Oh Marie ... Marie,
nobody loves you but me.

His songs were dark or funny, but always strange, about people with blood on their hands, men going frantic, men losing their thumbs and having toes reattached in their place: "They called this new appendage, they called it the thoe." He frowned when he sang, hung his head when he played. In his white T-shirt he was luminous. Again I noticed girls watching him and suspected they were falling in love with him. Still, whenever I watched the band play I was struck by a despair similar to that I'd felt when Big Red had entered the picture. I thought: Why isn't he famous? It was incredible that nothing great had happened yet. When would it happen, when? *Well, I don't know, Eyelash.*

Sometimes my parents came to these gigs. On my twentieth birthday the band played at a café. Rain was beating against the windows and they had to turn up their amplifiers to be heard. My father sat with folded arms in his Vodafone-branded bomber jacket. My mother sat beside him, not so much nodding her head as pitching it forward, every so often, to the music. She liked to call out. "Wonderful, John-Paul!" A boy I liked was there too, sitting at a table at the back drinking ginger beer. I wanted to talk to him alone—I knew he played the piano and was studying jazz, which I knew nothing about—but I also wanted the room to be filled with people, all of them drunken and euphoric, so they could see the band and see how great they were, how unlike anything else.

Before I started writing the piece I'd told JP about at the library that day, I searched for photographs of Big Red. I looked through the old chest in the garage at my parents' house. I found photographs of my brothers playing guitars in the living room at home, photos of tables covered in beer cans and CDs, photos of Neil with his hair dyed red, photos of JP and me playing the piano, photos of JP inexplicably wearing an inflatable travel pillow around his neck on Christmas Day—but no photographs of Big Red. The only picture I had of it was the one in my head.

I worried about the gaps in my knowledge. Writing about that time implied that I understood it—but the truth was that I had only ever really been a visitor, looking on, wishing. It had been my brothers' world, not mine. I remembered one of Neil's early short films, a high school assignment about the concept of change. Its title: *Change, by Neil Young.* The opening credits, over which a Spaz song played, started with a shot of Neil walking into the living room, looking around briefly, scratching his head, then walking out again. The next three shots were exactly the same, only he entered the room from different doorways, each time with increasing bewilderment. And then it was JP's turn to walk in. Neil's voice shouted, "Presenting . . . John-Paul Young!" JP walked into the room wearing Dad's long dressing gown. He nodded solemnly at the camera, as if meeting a dignitary, then walked out.

Finally, it was my turn. "Presenting: Ashleigh Young!" I walked into the room—for some reason wearing a long flowery nightie; why were we all in sleepwear, all the time?—and bowed stiffly before turning and walking out again. And that was that; it was time for the film to start. But as the picture and music were fading out—Neil was fond of the extended fadeout—you could clearly see me *walk into the room again.* I wasn't acting. I wasn't in on any joke. I was simply, mortifyingly confused about what I was supposed to be doing. I wandered off again just before the picture faded to black.

Was there any story I could tell that was truly certain? *Write*

your way toward an understanding, a tutor had told me in a creative writing class during my third year of university. But what if
you went backward and wrote yourself *away from* the understanding? Was it better then never to have started at all? If
you were uncertain, should you make the understanding up—
construct a meaningful-sounding statement so that your reader
wouldn't feel that you'd strung them along, wasted their time?

Despite my worry, the writing courses I'd taken gave me a
new confidence and a recklessness. I'd been warned against it,
but I found myself writing about my family. I believed that simply describing these people, especially at those times when they
were most mysterious to me, would show their faces to me more
clearly and bring me closer to them. I began with my parents.
Once, I knew, they had been in their twenties. I tried to describe
things exactly as I knew them: the songs they wrote, their parties, the "movie" they made in the late 1970s, soundtracked by
Bob Dylan songs, which I first watched on a scratchy VHS with
my brothers. The movie was filled with incongruous scenes:
There was my moustached father at a campsite, sword-fighting
his friend Hutch with a tent pole. There was a staging of an
Olympics javelin event in our backyard, which ended with my
father writhing around on the grass, a javelin sticking out of his
back. And then there they all were, on a train as it rounded a for-
ested coastline, my father alive and well again, his moustache
even more spirited. I had an urge to walk into those scenes. I
wanted to go back and find them.

And I wanted to find my brothers. For that, I had to find a
beginning: *Among the thicket of bush socks, duffel coat as black as*

a dog, and sticky woolen jumpers, there was the jacket, ready to be hoisted like a flag.

As I wrote, I realized that I'd thought and talked about the idea of the piece so much that it seemed almost to have gone and built itself without me. It existed separately from what was unfolding on my computer screen, which was not a story so much as something like one of Snake-Beings's shrines, made from detritus that clunks and flickers and has eyes that follow you around the house—but the whole doesn't fit together in any ordinary way. The story was also helplessly in my voice, which didn't seem right. I had always left the talking to my brothers. They were the ones with the driver's licenses. I sat in the backseat and never learned to drive.

And as I wrote more, I found that my two stories, my two strands of past and present—the story of my brother JP, and the story of myself writing it—began to overlap. I could no longer keep looking back on that time as if it were a story, because it was not a story, it was real, and anyway, whatever it was, it was not yet finished.

JP left the postal service and returned to work at IHC, which this time meant doing things like delivering Meals on Wheels. And Neil was preparing to finish his job as the editor of *Tearaway* magazine before he would go to London; I suspected I wouldn't see him again for years, not until we all were truly grown, not until we all shared my mother's legendary furrowed brow.

In the meantime, I was at university, reading Chaucer, or I was working behind a shop counter, or I was worrying about my boyfriend, the jazz pianist, whom I loved but whose moods frightened me and, perhaps worse, whose taste in music mystified me. I began to see less of JP. In all of my busyness I was becoming self-absorbed.

Maybe my distance from both my brothers helped me to see them more clearly. Maybe, in a cruel way, I could now think and write about them as characters, could detach myself and write things that were not truly my own.

JP wrote and recorded a solo album called *Jilted* after he and the beautiful girl broke up and she became engaged to a swimming coach. On the album's cover was a photo of him standing on a gray beach on the south coast of Wellington with his hands in his back pockets. I listened to the album on my headphones a lot. Walking to work, walking home, in my room. He'd recorded most of it on a four-track in his bedroom, but he recorded the piano for one song at my grandparents' farm in Oamaru. My grandmother's yellowing piano had a jangly saloon sound—I'd known it always as a "honky-tonk piano," because that's the kind of music our grandmother had played at social dances and clubs around that town—and he'd added a reverse effect that made it sound as if the notes were rushing past like cars. "I was really going for the broken-down feel," he explained. The album did sound broken down, but at the same time it was moving cautiously on, wheels slipping and sliding. And his voice was still slightly out of tune, in a way that always made me listen more carefully.

In the last song on the album, his friend Jane played the cello, a slow sawing. JP's voice was crackly as he sang.

> *Well it's the early days that I miss most*
> *when our love was young and sweet*
> *before the broken promises and the secrets we had to keep*
> *before the reckless love that freed us*
> *and in the end deceived us and led us on*
> *was gone, gone, gone*

Then he played the harmonica, a slow, mournful tune, and the song ended.

"Why don't you get a manager?"

"Why don't you hire out a proper recording studio?"

"You could always go back to uni."

I had this habit of offering up ideas and solutions when I met JP. It was my project, just as once I'd tried to persuade him to give up Big Red and wear something else. He'd react either by nodding and frowning very seriously as he twirled his spoon in his cup until all the milk froth was gone—"Oh, I don't know, Eyelash. It's just not really viable at this point in time"—or by nodding effusively: "That's a good idea! I'll make some inquiries." I suspected that he wouldn't get around to it. And after not getting around to it, too much time would have passed, until the idea was no longer any good.

I thought of how Neil was always telling me about an incredible band he'd just heard or a writer he had discovered. I inherited his bookshelves when he left for London, and Neil talked me through the collection. On the back covers of the books were men with hollow eyes and bad skin: Bukowski, Bellow, the Amises. He called them all brilliant. He idolized Nabokov in particular, and had a gigantic poster of him glaring vehemently down from the wall above his bed. These men were soon to line the walls of my small room in Aro Valley, and I was anxious to be as exhilarated as Neil had been by their monumental works.

Nothing quite left that kind of impression on JP. He seemed too tired to take much in. It was as if the world was slipping over him like water. If he could just get started again, I thought, and write some new songs, maybe a new album, get some good gigs with the right combination of people watching—then, like a gleaming wave, fame would pick him up and carry him forward. He just had to position himself correctly to catch it, if such a wave existed, if such a sea existed.

In his film *Change*, Neil had demonstrated some moments in which a person's circumstances change. First, he used a pair of old stockings to tie JP to a lemon tree in a field.

"Right now, he's dry," he said to the camera. Then he picked up a bucket of water and tipped it over JP's head. "Now, he is wet." He progressed through a few other contrasts—clean, dirty; not covered in flour, covered in flour. Then he poured liquid from a jerry can around the tree. "Right now he's not on fire," Neil quipped, striking a match; "soon, he will be." JP stood perfectly still, looking plaintive. After being lit on fire—which Neil indicated by borrowing an explosion scene from the first Terminator movie—JP miraculously survived, only to be covered in corn mash and eaten alive by the hens in the coop nearby. Again, I had a walk-on role—I had to wander into the coop and let out a scream upon discovering the body lying in the grass. (Of course, I messed it up again: instead of walking casually toward the coop's gate, I sprinted, gasping, somehow already knowing that a hen-pecked corpse awaited me there.)

It was meant to be funny, and it was, but there was something else about that scene that I kept coming back to. It captured—in an extreme way, of course—the way that JP never visibly put up a fight. He didn't struggle to free himself from the tie made of stockings; instead he stood patiently, waiting for the match to take, while Neil made a dramatic dive for safety. The corn mash must have been bitterly cold, yet there he lay in the grass, motionless, hens peering down at him.

At least, though, he was still playing music. He was now in a band he'd found through a "Singer/Guitarist Wanted" ad. But the band didn't quite jell. The drummer stared balefully into the audience, drowning out the rest of the band with his leaden crashing. The bassist danced badly and alone and at the wrong times. The only holdover from JP's former lineup, Raj, stood fixedly at one side of the stage with his guitar. JP wandered irritably around the stage, kicking at leads and fiddling with pedals. His singing took on a shouty quality, and he sometimes aborted songs partway through.

At one gig at Happy Bar, my mother came along. Between songs she called out proudly, "Wonderful, John-Paul!"

"Thanks, Mum," he said into the microphone.

"That's not very rock 'n' roll," someone in the crowd jeered.

JP suddenly glared into the lights. "Oh, yeah?" he said. "Well, how about—*fuck you, motherfucker.*" Then he released a piercing round of feedback from his guitar. "Always good to get feedback, don't you think?" His bandmates howled with laughter; a few people in the audience laughed, but a few others started to leave.

In a Clampers song called "Fly by Nighters" is the line "I'd do it all in pastel grays, I'd mute the page and speak in slow motion." It was an upbeat song, but lines like that made me think of a mind in which color could suddenly disappear, all forward motion could slow. "The black turned gray and drained away to an old house and a leaden sky."

Behind the numbness, the dead calm, was a sort of panic bubbling away. Once, on a visit to a friend in Auckland, JP found himself sitting in someone's backyard, in the garden, somewhere he didn't know, crying. He felt unstable, he told me later, and the tentative way he said it, as if uncertain it was the right word, made me think of a tottering physical structure. I thought of the Flying Fox we'd tried to build together in a tall tree decades before; JP had fallen into thick thorny shrubs below the tree, cast out of the ice cream container we'd used, feebly, as a seat.

Seeing a counselor didn't help him much. "I did an awful lot of talking about how I felt, and things from the past—but it didn't lead to anything. It just made me feel drained and horrible at the end of each hour, and I'd be dumped back out on the street. Then I ran out of sessions, and I couldn't afford to keep going."

For the first time, I understood that JP had stories that perhaps would never be shared, that others might never touch—

except, perhaps, for what he told in songs, obliquely. Many of his songs were written from the perspective of damaged or washed-up characters who were somehow trapped in themselves, like the murder ballad where an obsessed lover kills a man, or "Real-life Superhero," which plays out the gulf between a man's self-delusion and his grim reality. Or "Buddy Holly Glasses," a harrowing song about a boy who is kidnapped. A version of this had happened to JP himself in Auckland, following a trip on the *Spirit of New Zealand*; after driving him aimlessly around the city for an hour, the kidnapper had relented and let him out— unlike in the song, which ends with the boy's murder. Once, at a party, someone asked him to play a few songs, and JP took out his guitar and played the song about the kidnapper and the murder. There was total silence when he finished; then all the guests shifted and laughed nervously and someone said, "So, wow." It was the first time I'd heard the song, too, and I couldn't think what to say. Finally JP cleared his throat, said, "Well! That's enough of that," and launched into "Tangled Up in Blue."

Things from the past were bigger when you were at a low ebb. Sometimes there was a ghost standing by your bed, not saying a word. Sometimes you woke up from a nightmare paralyzed, pinned to your bed as if someone were sitting on your chest. Moments from decades earlier could accost you all of a sudden, like being tied to a tree and being lit on fire or having a bucket of water thrown at you.

I was ashamed of myself, now, for asking so insistently what I could do with stories I only half understood. I stopped writing about Big Red and all that I wanted it to symbolize. I left university and picked up some freelance work writing stories for a publisher of children's books, which allowed me to invent characters completely and to research things like the history of airplanes and the story of Amelia Earhart. It was a relief to make things up or simply to retell famous histories. I stopped writing about my family, except in poems, where I was able to come at things sideways, to examine only fragments. The poems came out of other, harmless memories that I knew were fully mine: the long hallway of our house, the pear tree on the sloping lawn, the black dog running, JP crash-landing in the shrubs, and me watching from the tall tree.

> *Closets full of skeletons, rattling round and causin' mayhem*
> *People bury hatchets deep, they're pickin' the bones like hyenas*
> *Canyons full of broken rocks*
> *Bridges burnin' far behind me*
>
> —The Clampers, "Disarray"

Neil left for London, where he spent his days typing and nights furtively drinking Champagne and red wine at hospitality functions he worked as a waiter. He wrote about going running through Clapham and being dive-bombed by crows. His emails reassured me that the world outside of New Zealand was still just the world, only in slightly different configurations. People had jobs and ate meals and got drunk and fell in love out there. It wasn't automatically special by virtue of being far away.

And JP flew to Denver. He got a job as a shuttle driver for Colorado Mountain Express, driving tourists, musicians, and hockey stars from the airport to ski lodges in the mountains. He hadn't been to America before, and he wrote to me about traveling through Las Vegas. "It seemed like a lonely place somehow," he said, "a blinking bleeping oasis in the middle of a frozen desert."

> Some of the casinos were diabolically lavish—one had a replica of the Trojan horse and canals (complete with barges) going through it. After a while, though, they all began to look the same. There's only so many ways you can disguise the hungry slots of those poker machines, I suppose.
>
> And amidst the glitter, there were shambolic bedraggled figures—beggars rattling cups.

Unlike the world Neil described in his emails, when JP described where he was, it was no longer just the world. It really was somewhere else. He wrote about luminous snowy mountains, and days so cold that his keys froze inside his pocket, and going "nocturnal snowshoeing," walking along the surface of a frozen river with some friends.

> At one point I took a step and fell up to my waist in snow and when I finally managed to drag myself free, I was missing a snowshoe. After a half hour spent miserably prodding at snow banks with assorted sticks, we trudged home.

In my postgraduate year at university, I wrote a thesis on the poems of Frank O'Hara. I returned to his lines over and over. I found recordings of him reading his poems—I loved his accent, the way you could imagine him bursting out laughing, the way you could imagine what he was like with his friends. The poem I especially loved was "Adieu to Norman, Bon Jour to Joan and Jean-Paul":

> the only thing to do is simply continue
> is that simple
> yes, it is simple because it is the only thing to do
> can you do it
> yes, you can because it is the only thing to do

What were the ways in which to continue? Obviously getting up in the morning was one way. Getting dressed, facing people around you. These were the ways that kept your life open to possibility. But there was another way of continuing. It was the continuing of silence. Our family had always continued to continue through events that we did not know how to speak of to one another. It was caused, perhaps, by a combination of exhaustion and limited vocabulary. It meant that always, for instance, following an argument between my parents and my father locked out of the house, morning would come and the things that had fallen apart would slide almost imperceptibly together again, until they had returned to normal, or at least, to the way they had been before. The faint hairline cracks that ran over each day could be passed over. They became part of us; we smoothed them over with routine.

While part of me was relieved at a silence that allowed us to move further and further away from darkness, another part of me was unconvinced that whatever we'd ignored would go away for good. It was as if we wished to place events under sedation. One of my father's favorite songs was Pink Floyd's "Comfortably Numb"; I remember him singing it in his high, thin voice. Despite his singing, we all liked that song.

As JP and I exchanged emails, the subject of his unhappiness receded as if of its own volition, and from a distance, we did continue. His life filled up with another country. The mountains were terrifying and dazzling. At an empty airfield, he and the other drivers learned how to drive their vans—how to accelerate into corners, coast on the brakes, slide along the treacherously smooth tarmac. The others working at Colorado Mountain Express were mostly Australians, New Zealanders, and Americans. When off duty, the nights began with beer and guitars, and ended with spaghetti trampled into the carpet and doors hanging off their hinges.

> Today I drove home with some stressed-out Polish people in the back of the van. They were getting angry about the amount of luggage on board, which was all theirs. It was a Seinfeldian scene at the airport—I felt like Kramer, frantically hammering the door shut on a bulging pile of suitcases while this bald geezer muttered recriminations at me. It was reminiscent of some of the wilder days of Meals on Wheels.

The other day Richard Dean Anderson was at Eagle Airport—all faded jeans and thinning hairline. He looked pretty cool, but I kept my distance. You shouldn't get too close to your heroes.

It's funny, the things that were niggling at my mind have receded. Time has slowed down, and all that nonsense seems very far away.

Then there was an accident—a skidding on ice. JP's van whirled and spun off the highway, crashing into a snowbank. I could only imagine it, just as I had imagined the crumpled Cortina, the cows on the road. I imagined JP emerging slowly from the van, as if in a scene from *Terminator*, wincing as he pulled himself upright, testing his legs. Mercifully, nothing exploded into flames behind him. The van was empty of passengers; JP had already deposited them safely at their hotels. He surveyed the buckled hood, the front tires buried in snow, and rang for help. Then he waited on the side of the highway. You could train for what to do before a crash—you could practice sliding and whirling around an empty airfield. But you couldn't practice for waiting for help. When the tow truck came to haul JP's van out of the snow, he saw that only a hundred or so meters down the highway was a yawning crevasse.

After the crash I was quite a shambles for a few days. I'm in a convalescent haze, as Beck would say. I suppose if it makes me more careful and aware of how fragile everything is, maybe it was a good thing—though, dammit, I already knew that! I can't go getting myself killed over here. I want to get back home too much.

Shortly thereafter, JP was home to stay. The first time we saw him again, he was wearing a puffy ski jacket, which he'd zipped up to the neck so that his face loomed large and craggy over the top. It was still the same face, if deeper around the eyes. Neil was home too, over from London for a visit, and as we waited for our food I saw him looking at the new jacket with his own eyes slightly narrowed.

The café we were in was largely empty. We spent some time taking photos of one another and grinning into the large gilded mirror on the wall. Both of my brothers looked taller after their time spent overseas, and were more urgent in their stride, as if eager to get away again. Over our dinner JP told us about meeting the Beach Boys and driving them through a snowstorm to a hotel in the small town of Avon.

"They looked fagged out," he said. "They were trapped on the greatest-hits purgatory treadmill, I guess. The keyboard player said he'd been playing the same thing for ten years."

"It must've been cool to meet them, though," Neil said.

"It was—although I must say it was a sobering experience." He described the various afflictions of Brian and Dennis and Mike, and how the band these days was mostly fill-in members, how they'd all sat silently in the back of the van looking frayed at the edges.

Neil took a photo of us standing in front of Star Takeaways on Riddiford Street. We are two grayish figures standing uncertainly in front of the shop window, as if caught in a fade-out shot in one of Neil's films.

JP and I spent Christmas Day in the city. We biked through the Mount Victoria Tunnel, and when we came out the other side it was raining. We rode around the bay a short way, ringing our bells at lone runners, then headed up a gradual slope into a growing headwind. JP rode fast. I kept my eyes on his back, his billowing black jacket, as though keeping him in my line of sight would pull me forward, even as I slipped farther and farther behind.

In Wellington in 2009, JP started a degree in music therapy. As part of his degree he ran classes for young people with behavioral difficulties. He gave them drums and pipes and bells and many other instruments: ukuleles, glockenspiels, tambourines, a xylophone, a gourd-shaped percussion instrument called a güiro, a mandolin, a battered electric keyboard, bongo drums, twelve-string guitars, an African thumb piano, egg shakers, maracas, cowbells, ordinary hand bells, and Boomwhackers. These last were eight brightly colored lengths of plastic, each tuned to a note in C major. They could be used to play melodies and rhythms at the same time, but the students used them mostly for sword fighting. Sometimes the group wrote songs and recorded them; sometimes they just sat and listened to their favorite songs. Nearly always it was chaotic, but it couldn't be any other way, and JP was as fearless as he'd ever been. Finally he'd found a kind of work that he liked and was good at. "When you put a bunch of kids with behavioral problems in a room with a pile of instruments, things can get out of hand." He was full of maxims for music therapy. "It's always good to pick up new instruments, but it can be an expensive and heavy business."

Whenever JP talked about his classes, I'd think of a group of kids I'd once seen performing in Civic Square. They were whacking drums, shaking rattles, honking on recorders, and stamping their feet. They had a conductor, a gray-haired man beaming at his students as he clapped his hands over his head. There was no rhythm or melody, but the noise was continuous. It sounded like a huge vehicle lurching down a road. It was hard to tell what the performance was building toward—if it was building toward anything—but I stood and watched for a few minutes. As I listened closely, I began to hear the music inside the noise. It was possible to pick out single instruments—a drum, a triangle, a recorder rippling up and down a scale or stalled on one happy note. I thought I could detect a shape, then a movement, something speeding toward a blasting finale.

Once JP described a new student, a teenager he was trying to teach guitar. The teenager wasn't very interested in learning, but JP persisted. "When he looks at you he has this sort of frozen expression on his face, and I always think, What's he seeing when he looks at me?" He sounded both curious and slightly fearful as he imagined what it could be.

We are walking through Newtown, Wellington, pushing bikes. JP looks squinty and fuzzy-headed. Last night he played some of his new songs at Mighty Mighty. He is pushing a muddy black Raleigh, his girlfriend's bike. I ask where Big Red is—the new Big Red, his ten-speed Healing, which is a true American-sunset red, but with rust speckling the rims of its wheels and black foam furling out of the ends of its handlebars.

"He's still out of action. The gear cable snapped. Bloody Jeff tried to fix it but ended up brutalizing it."

Jeff is a cyclist who recently rode with JP and another friend, Kohe, to Whanganui, a small city, sleeping in parks and camp-grounds along the way. At a spot along a river, Jeff insisted on trying to catch an eel with a pair of pants, knotting the legs and floating bread inside the waistband in the hopes that an unsus-pecting eel would swim inside. No eels did, but it seemed that anything was possible. There is a photo of them with their bikes at Levin Railway Station in the sun, muscled legs in shorts, all grinning. JP's caption reads *Bromance*.

We get talking about the perils of cycling in Wellington. I ask, "What's your policy on red lights?"

"Well, it really depends. If it's a big intersection I'll wait, but if it's for a pedestrian crossing I'll ride up on the footpath then ride back onto the road after the red light."

"So you break two laws instead of one!"

"Yes, but . . . I feel like riding on the footpath is a lesser evil than hamfistedly running a red light."

He plays solo now. He uses a sampler with distortion pedals, a guitar and a harmonica and sometimes a kazoo. Jane the cellist accompanies him on some of the songs. His friend Vorn plays the accordion, violin, or theremin, making a sound like gulls wheeling. The songs build up piece by piece, with the percussion escalating into an erratic racket. These new songs are still strange and bleak, or bleakly funny.

> *Like a washed-up carcass on a lonesome beach*
> *A worm eatin' out the middle of a peach*
> *Something hanging just out of reach*
> *Your love is a part of me babe*
> *Your love is a part of me babe*

But the songs seem to belong even more to JP now, and his voice has become stronger and more commanding. And when he's in front of the sampler, and the song is properly kicking in, he'll suddenly start to dance—lurching side to side, shooting his arms in all directions, a stern look on his face as he gyrates.

JP walks with me up to the intersection, where he'll turn around and ride out to Island Bay to visit a friend. A strong northerly is blowing, so he'll have a tailwind riding south. Before he goes, he says he is going to get Big Red fixed soon, in time for summer.

Then he fastens his helmet and says, "See you later, Eyelash!" He rings the bell and rides off down the road.

window seat

At 8:20 on Thursday morning I found my seat, the middle of the row over the wing of the plane, sat down, and switched on my Kindle. I was reading *The Examined Life*, Stephen Grosz's account of his experiences as a psychoanalyst, and I had reached the last section, "Leaving," in which Grosz has taken on a new patient, a young man, who has just been diagnosed with HIV. The young man is beginning to spend all of his psychoanalysis sessions in deep, still, heavy silence, sometimes even falling asleep. I was at the part where Grosz is describing the different kinds of silences that patients sometimes bring to him—silences of refusal, discomfort, repression—when a tiny withered woman with a huge puffy black bag over her shoulder indicated she had the window seat beside me. I got up and helped her maneuver her bag into the overhead compartment, then she sat down and set about making herself comfortable; she took off her shoes, revealing papery brown feet, and arranged a blanket beneath her seat so that her feet had a resting place—her legs, in leopard-print leggings, were too short to reach the floor. She took out her own Kindle, which was in a proper zippered case, and I went back to Grosz and the young man in the therapy room.

"Under ordinary circumstances," Grosz was saying, "I might ask a patient who has been silent for some time what they're thinking or feeling, and once or twice I did this with Anthony. But I soon realised that my speaking was an intrusion, a disturbance." I stopped reading then because I couldn't focus. I was getting a sense of slight but building pressure between the window-seat woman and myself. It was a sense that she was about to say something, that she wasn't really going to read; she was just fiddling with the device while she decided where she would start with me. Sure enough.

"If you see me popping pills or dragging on an inhaler, don't you worry." She had a bright Queensland accent, with an unexpected burr, almost Scottish-sounding. "Bronchiectasis. Much worse than asthma. Had it for years and years, so I've got all these scars on my lungs. Big knotty scars. Bronchiectasis. Last time I left New Zealand I took this sickness with me; now I'm going to give the bloody thing back!" She motioned at her tiny chest. "I've had about a hundred pneumonias and a fair few oper-ations. It was all the mold in New Zealand. That's why I moved away to Australia. But I'm tough. Don't worry if you see me puff-ing away."

She looked at me sideways. She had blue eyes in a small tanned face, and one of those open-mouthed smiles that made it look as though she was silently saying "Aaah!" She pulled a plas-tic lunch container out of the front seat pocket, cracked open the lid, and took out an egg sandwich, which she ate while swinging her feet and looking out the window. We were right above the wing. Outside on the tarmac an electric cart was shut-tling about, a figure in high-vis at the wheel. "Sometimes when you're between New Zealand and Australia," she said between mouthfuls, "if you look down you can see a rainbow circle in the sea. A glassy sort of rainbow, like a big bowl. I always get the window seat so I can see it, because it's beautiful. But we won't be able to see it with that darn wing there." I said it was a shame about the wing, and she said, "No, not a shame, it's just the way it's happened."

She was quiet for a while, and in the meantime another el-derly woman sat down in the aisle seat, to my left. She was dressed in shimmery black clothing and had white-blue hair, and bronzer on her cheekbones. She had the look of a dulled but beautiful gemstone, maybe an opal. (As I was thinking about what sort of gemstone she'd be, I remembered how in Brisbane I'd thought aloud that the crows—huge and formidable, picking their way about the streets—had eyes that looked like sequins. My friend James said, "Maybe the eyes have evolved to look like sequins, because crows know that humans like the look of sequins." We'd laughed and then fallen into our usual too-easy silence as we walked along.) I helped the opal woman adjust the direction of the tiny fan above us so that it was blowing directly into her hair; then we sat down. I was probably a frustrating barrier between the two women, making it less likely that they would talk to each other, when they might have more to say to each other—but then a middle-aged woman came down the aisle and handed the opal woman a packet of jelly beans. "You'll need these for energy, Mum." Her mother thanked her and tucked the jelly beans away, then reclined her seat and put her sleeping mask on.

"Last time I flew, I got terrible altitude sickness," the window-seat woman whispered to me. "It was years ago. I remember lying on the floor under the seats thinking I might be dying. Suddenly the word 'God' came to me. 'God, God, God, God.' I felt like the word was beaming into me right down the center, like a torch beam, filling me with the word 'God,' and I thought, Well, if this is dying, it's all right." That must have been incredibly stressful, I said, and she jutted her chin upward, squinting. "It's how it happened, and it got me to where I needed to be." She looked out at the wing. "This is the first time I've flown in many, many years." The Scottish burr again. "I haven't been able to, with my sickness. But if I make it this time, it's a sign I'll be able to make it to Switzerland, where my son lives. This is my test flight, you see." She gave the open-mouthed smile again. "I'm meeting my sister in Wellington. First time I've seen her in five years. We were born in Invercargill. I had to leave because of the mold." Then she told me about the first time she'd been up in a plane, when she was sixteen. Her friend's father was a pilot, and he had a small plane. They all went up together in the small plane and did acrobatics for half an hour. "Straight after the flight, my friend and I went off to a dance. All dressed up in our miniskirts. I was feeling so sick. My very first dance, I vomited all over my partner! He was very annoyed with me."

We were still on the tarmac, and I was already feeling tired, because even though I'd enjoyed listening to the woman's stories, I'd had to react with surprise and delight at them. My energy for talking to strangers gets depleted quickly. Maybe sitting next to window-seat woman would be too much. But she was quiet now, and soon we were in the air, and Brisbane, with its pale sky and all its evenly tanned people in sunglasses and sleeveless tops, was dropping away. Window-seat woman nudged me and said, "Look." She had something in her hand. It was a white rock with corrugated, granular swirls in it, the swirls like the movements of a worm or a centipede. It looked like it could be a fossil. "I couldn't resist picking this up on the beach early this morning. Nature! I don't suppose they'll let me through with it." How had she gotten it through customs? I started to laugh. I said I didn't think they would let her through when we landed with the rock. "Well, it's here now," she said, and put it back in her bag with satisfaction.

I had been up since quarter to five because I'd had to walk to the train station with James, who was flying back to Darwin. I closed my eyes and fell into a blank doze. When I opened them again I felt heavy and sad. I always feel a bit sad on flights between countries. I can't help thinking about the past and the future and where I will end up. The geographical limbo seems to emphasize a limbo I feel in myself. I was staring into space, thinking about all this, when the woman suddenly said, "My brother's a cross-dresser," and I was jolted back into our little row. "Been doing it for ten years, and has never been happier," she said. "He'd always felt pulled in all directions as a young man—he just wasn't ever himself. What grief. Imagine it. And when he was fifty, he met this wonderful woman who told him to just let go. Just let it out. And he started dressing like a woman, these lovely skirts, colorful shoes, and he and this woman who'd told him to do it, they ended up married. It was a real eye-opener for our whole family. We all loved him, but now we had to learn how to love him as a lady, too."

I got the sense she'd told the story numerous times but that she liked to tell it because it confirmed something she'd long believed about people and about their true selves. "It's an amazing way to have your whole world opened up, you know." She prised another sandwich from her plastic container and started to eat. We were flying over the clouds now, and were quiet again for a time.

When the opal woman took off her mask and shakily stood to make her way toward the toilets, I stood up too. The window-seat woman followed. Ordinarily I would've felt irritated, but with this woman I didn't. She didn't seem needy or searching with her stories. She didn't seem to expect anything from me. She would have told the same stories to whoever was seated beside her. We queued together at the end of the aisle, while the people in the toilets took what seemed like a very long time. Window-seat woman looked at me incredulously. "Funny how some people take so long. Just like life, isn't it?" Then she looked fixedly at me and said: "About forty years ago my brother—not the cross-dresser one, the other one—was flying over Saudi Arabia, and the plane got hijacked. It was in the days when it was easy to hijack a plane. The hijackers made the pilots land in a desert." The thought crossed my mind then that the woman could be lying, at least exaggerating. "They had to stay there for two days until they were rescued. My brother was fine in the end, and no one was killed. But he came back to us very much older." She gave a strange, sad laugh. "And later on, he ended up dying of AIDS. What a mystery." A toilet door finally opened and she went in while I stayed waiting in the aisle. I thought about the woman's brother, and about the young man lying silently on the couch in the psychoanalyst's office. It had taken Grosz a long time to understand that all Anthony needed was not to feel alone. He didn't need to talk, but he wanted to fall asleep without fear, knowing that when he was gone he stayed present and alive in the mind of another.

Back in our seats, it wasn't long before the woman spoke again, and for the next twenty minutes she told me that she'd once been a bikie in the Hells Angels—had probably been one of New Zealand's first female bikies—but got in trouble with the police so had to give it up; that she'd been thrown out of numerous nightclubs as a youngster because her skirt was too short; that once she went to an auction at Lyall Bay and her young daughter had tripped over in front of her, and when she reached out to pick her up she made a particular motion that made the auctioneer think she was bidding, and she ended up buying a big oak table. She told me that it was in Lower Hutt when her real life began, because it was here that she realized she was a healer.

What happened was this: A friend had arrived in Lower Hutt

after a long flight, and he had hurt his elbow lifting a heavy suit-case. She had put her hands on his elbow to rub it and comfort him, and when she did, something happened.

"I felt this strange, powerful tingling in my hands and arms, and I thought I must be getting pins and needles. After a few moments, I had this strong feeling that my friend's elbow was better now. I took my hands away, and he said, 'Gosh, my elbow feels much better.' I said to myself, I'm a healer, I'm a healer!" She said that many years later, she ended up with her own healing practice in Zurich. Her husband earned all the money, so she didn't charge for her healing services.

It was possible that she was recklessly inventing. Who easier to tell an imagined life to than a stranger on a plane whom you'll likely never see again? The geography and timescale of her life was erratic—she had mentioned Invercargill, suburbs around Wellington, Paekākāriki, all over Europe, all over Australia—and it was hard to figure out who she was without being able to connect her firmly to one particular place. The past seemed so vivid to her that it was also hard for me to grasp that some of the stories she was telling took place more than forty years ago. I made up my mind not to decide there and then whether she was telling the truth. I wanted to stay open for as long as I could.

I was wide-awake when she said, with resolve: "Now, I'm going to tell you about you." She had not expressed any particular interest in me until this point, beyond asking me how old I was and what I did for a living. Opal woman was having a close, whispered conversation with her daughter, who had come down the aisle again holding a miniature hairbrush.

"You love your cat," the window-seat woman said; "you love your cat very much, and you love all animals," and then I realized that she must think she had psychic abilities, along with healing abilities. There was nothing to do but play along; I was trapped here. I told her she was right about the cat and the animals. "You're very gentle," she went on. "At your core you are very gentle, though you can be spiky on the outside." How does one disagree? Isn't that the basic human condition?

"Where do you live . . . ? I'm seeing you living on the top of a hill. Steep hill. And you're zipping about on the roads, very quick, very zippy. An explorer." She motioned with her hands.

"You're very like your mother but you think she talks too much. Your father is a bit hazy to me." She frowned for a while. "You have more of a connection with one of your brothers than the other one, perhaps." Then she shook her head. "I could go on and on, but it wouldn't do either of us any good." She laughed and said, "I will just say, I don't see any black marks ahead. Isn't that great!" She peered at me. "I also will just say, you need to clean your glasses."

We spent some time in quiet. I tried to read my book again. Anthony had not died—in fact, after being told he might have two years left and that essentially he had no future, he had lived for a very long time. "I now think that Anthony's silences expressed different things at different times," Grosz was saying.

"Sorrow, a desire to be close to me but stay separate, and a wish to stop time." Anthony was still alive at the chapter's close, and then I began a new chapter, about a woman named Alice P., who was trying to grieve for a baby she had lost, but wasn't able to.

We were ten minutes from landing when the woman turned to me and said, "I wanted to save this till the very end. I see some big changes ahead for you. Your life is going to go like that." She made a zigzaggy motion with her hand. "Yes, you've spent so much time putting others first, and it's your turn now." She looked at me with such kindness that I put aside, for a moment, the knowledge that this is what psychics routinely tell their charges, because this is what people want to hear. Everyone wants to feel chosen. Being told "it's your turn now" feels like being praised, or needed, or pursued. But then she said, drily, "I don't suppose you've met the love of your life." I was flustered and felt a surge of annoyance. It was her knowingness, and her flippancy. I told her, "I'm not sure I believe in that expression 'love of your life.' But I feel that maybe I have, actually, back home." She said, "Well, let's see. You're at the perfect age. Women come right at your age. Men never really come right." I got really annoyed then—maybe she would go on to ask someone else if they had found the love of their life, and that person would grow doubtful about all of their decisions and throw everything away—and turned on my Kindle and read that Grosz's sister had been to speak to a clairvoyant when she had lost her home and all her possessions in a brush fire in California. Grosz's sister said that through the clairvoyant she'd spoken to her and Grosz's mother, who had been dead for more than twenty years, and Grosz was surprised to find himself tearful. "What did Mom say?"

We were descending quickly into Wellington now and I could see the hills and houses taking on their familiar edges. The pilot had just announced that the local temperature was 12 degrees Celsius—about 54 Fahrenheit—with a strong southerly, and a shriek had gone up from all the Queenslanders on board. I finished my book, and found myself crying. Window-seat woman murmured, "Jerry must be missing you." Jerry is the name of my cat. She said, "Is that his name? Jerry? He'll be glad to see you." I managed to say, "Yes, yes it is," even as I was shaking my head. At some point I must have said Jerry's name, I must have, but as I combed carefully back through our conversation, I was sure I hadn't.

After we landed and were waiting for the seat belt sign to turn off, she said to me, "Do they still call Wellington the City of Angels? They always said that the angels help planes to get down safely to the ground." I said no, I was sure they had never called it that. Then I helped her to pull her bag from the overhead compartment and a few minutes later she was swallowed by the steadily moving line of passengers ahead of me.

black dog book

Christina and Black Dog are best friends—until
Christina catches sight of a strange and wonderful
bird high up in the treetops, and from then on can
think of nothing else. Black Dog longs to show
Christina how much he still loves her. And so he
decides to take an enormous risk.
—*Blurb for* Black Dog *by Pamela Allen*

One set of neighbors has a little black-and-white dog tied to a chair on the lawn. When I call through the fence, the dog wags its whole bottom, its tail petrified between its legs. Another dog, a dirty brown thing, lies on a patch of concrete nearby, eyebrows twitching. The house has all of its white curtains drawn. I extend my hand through a gap in the fence, beckoning, but the dogs don't come.

The neighbors adjacent to our house own a Rottweiler, a dark ripple through a gap in the corrugated iron between our properties. When the dog barks it sounds as if it's got a mouthful of barbed wire. Not far from its kennel is a cockatoo, which can say "Hello" and "Gidday," and does so at random throughout the day. These sounds seem to enrage the Rottweiler, who lunges about, dragging its chain against its enclosure. When I jump on the trampoline in our backyard I try to get a good look at the two animals, but I can't see much. The dark bulk of the Rottweiler. A flash of white feathers and yellow crest.

Over our back fence lives Joe, a yellow collie, owned by the Joyces. The Joyces shout at one another and at Joe. They are a shouting family. Added to the shouting is the chainsawing. Mr. Joyce cuts down trees late at night with his chainsaw. Something outside their house is always being broken or smashed or is crying. When the five o'clock siren sounds, Joe howls—a long ascension then descension, like a trombone—and one of the Joyces shouts, "Shut up, Joe!" This is followed by the snaking metal sound of Joe's chain as he retreats to his kennel. I daydream about rescuing him from the Joyces. I unclip the chain from his collar and carry him in a yielding bundle over the fence. I unbuckle his collar and rub the sore patches around his neck. I fill a bucket with soapy water and give him a bath and dry him gently with a towel. I give him something to eat, a leg of chicken. I make a sheepskin bed for him; I go to sleep in a chair beside him. My rescue fantasy for Joe is similar to what I'd once dreamed of doing for Laika, the stray dog who was chosen to be launched into space in 1957. A teacher at school told me that Laika would have enjoyed her adventure, but I know it's not true—that they'd all known she would die, that one of the technicians kissed her nose before closing her hatch.

All the dogs in the neighborhood live unlucky lives, except for mine.

Her head is as delicate as an overturned teacup. Her mouth holds many teeth, just white droplets still. My father's hand covers her face. Her eyes, glancing side to side, peer out between his hairy fingers. My brother shows how you can push back the skin on her forehead to make her look like Cleopatra. As we laugh at her, the dog lifts her chin high and regards us with cool slanted eyes, shaming us all.

My mother holds a party at our house, and men like Mr. McVinnie and Mr. Tutty arrive—tall men who conduct orchestras and choirs at the local high school. When the dog sees them she starts to tremble. To the dog, all men are electric. She slides onto her belly, then wriggles across the floor toward a man's shoes, pumping her neck like a swan, eyes shining.

Of all men, it is my father who has the greatest effect on the dog. From her belly position, she looks up at him—his huge leather shoes, his knees, his face—and her head quivers as if a current runs through her. My father stands motionless above her and they eyeball each other, as if something is passing between them in a slow curve.

"Woof," my father says suddenly, "woof." Then, straight-faced, he bobs up and down at the knees. What is this? Who is he being?

At this, the dog loses herself. She goes limp, flops to her side, and exposes her pink belly. Always my father ignores this cue.

Instead of bending down to stroke her belly, he bends down and spins her around on her back on the linoleum, like a dial on a spinboard.

My mother swoops in. "The wee lady. The wee bird." And she scoops the dog into her arms.

A miniature dachshund is very scoopable. It curls into your arms and becomes the shape of a croissant. The dog is always being picked up and put down and picked up again, and each time she gazes up meekly as she is molded to a new set of arms.

I creep into the washhouse late at night to settle her. We have placed her basket there, in this enclosed space with a sliding door. My guidebook on dachshunds recommends placing a small ticking clock into a puppy's bed to replicate the heartbeat of its mother, but I don't have a ticking clock, so there is no process by which I can soften the blow of having taken her away from her mother. Every night she whimpers. How can such a small dog, really only a bit bigger than a ball of wool, know so much about misery? When I open the door to the washhouse, she stops whimpering, scrambles out of her basket, and springs up on her hind legs. I take her paws to comfort her, and suddenly, I wish she wasn't there, I wish she was somebody else's, and I start to cry. I had wanted her at the house in Huntly, after we'd answered the ad in the newspaper, when she was a tiny black seed firing around the backyard with five other tiny black seeds. But I hadn't imagined this—being here alone with her, late at night, with her staring up and wanting.

The washhouse is cold: the window over the sink doesn't close, and at the other end of the room is a deep hollow in the wall, a kind of tub, stacked up with damp logs and sprigs of kindling, which gives the room a cobwebby smell, like inside a hedge. The dog's bed, a cane basket and old sheepskin, looks like the fallen nest of a strange bird.

I begin to look forward to coming into the washhouse every night to settle the dog and cry. In the washhouse I gather as much as I can into my sadness; my sadness is a magnet in my chest pulling everything into it, my sadness is a giant dog with loose folds of skin; I hug it to me. Then I let the real, tiny dog lick the salt off my face. Her paws scratch me as she leaps, and for a moment then my feeling of failure goes away.

One night, back in bed after my visit to the washhouse, I hear whispers. "Out you go. Hurry up." *Click-click-click* as the dog trots out to pee on the lawn. Then the soft scuffing of her paws as she pads up the hallway behind my mother to bed.

The dog may defer to my father, but she doesn't love him in the way she loves my mother. It's my mother who feeds her toast crusts in the mornings and tells her what's for dinner that night, how Japanese class has gone that day, whether my father is in trouble, what kind of wine she is opening. Before bed it's my mother who cradles her. The dog's black tail curls like a monkey's down my mother's nightie. The dog is "old goose," "wee bird," or "dogget." The dog is given permission to lick my mother's chin or put a wet nose into her eye.

"Mum! Don't let her do that!"

She buries her face in the dog's neck. "Oh, she's all right. Isn't she? Yes, yes. She's got a lovely *biscuity* smell today."

The dog does smell biscuity—malt biscuits, arrowroot biscuits. And she smells of the kitchen in our house: sponges, tea towels, a watery rust.

At night now, she sleeps between my parents, as if she were a much younger sibling of mine. I know this isn't right. My handbook has told me to have a hard heart. Before bed you should lock the pup in her designated night place with only her water bowl and basket. Put her in her bed and tell her to stay. If you leave her alone for long enough, she'll realize you are not going to save her. She'll become less frightened of being on her own and will respect you for your resilience and herself for her bravery. Of course I've failed these first tests. But I wouldn't go so far as to let her sleep in my bed. Now there's no hope of redemption.

"Say good night to the wee lady," my mother tells me as she stands in the doorway of my bedroom with the dog hugged to her chest. "Good night! Good night!"

I think of the ending of *Charlotte's Web*, when Wilbur looks up at Charlotte's children taking flight on their silken parachutes and hears their tiny voices farewelling him.

The dog looks as if she is a part of my mother, another head on her shoulders. "Good night."

The dogs inside books blur together in a fast-moving pack. A Saint Bernard keeps an Inuit girl warm when a snowstorm buries her. Again and again I come back to the simple line drawing of the girl enfolded by the dog; she is smiling slightly as she is warmed in the snow. A bull terrier and a Labrador retriever walk thousands of miles through the wilderness, eating frogs and fighting wildcats. A black mongrel and a fox terrier that wears a funny hat escape from a laboratory and are hunted through the countryside. A German shepherd is abandoned on a beach and is rescued by a young boy—they run everywhere together, and the boy teaches the dog to read, holding up signs that say "Sit" and "Stay." A genetically engineered golden retriever not only learns to read but learns to write; he also does battle with a fearsome monster that's half baboon and half tiger. And somewhere I see a painting of a woman with full frilly skirts, sitting on a chair with her hands crossed and a tiny black dog at her feet.

The picture book *Black Dog* by Pamela Allen at first seems to be about the friendship between a young girl named Christina and her dog. Christina loves Black Dog; Black Dog loves her back. But something strange happens: Christina becomes obsessed by a bird that's sitting in a tree outside. In the pictures she presses her face to the window each day, trying to see the bird again. She begins to neglect Black Dog, who grows thinner, lonelier, sadder, till his bones show through his coat. And this is how the story continues.

In the end, the desperate Black Dog tries to get Christina's attention back by throwing himself from the top of a pine tree. It works: Christina thinks she sees the bird at first, and then, in horror, she sees recognizes Black Dog as he falls. Is he trying to become like the mythical bird of Christina's dreams? Or is he so unhappy he is trying to kill himself? On the last page of the book Christina hugs her old, broken dog with love and regret. He looks peaceful and it's not clear whether he is alive or dead.

"Girl! Girl! Is that a sausage dog?"

I'm on the riverbank, walking the dog. My socks feel huge around my ankles. My shorts are too tight. I can't bear to be looked at and I can't bear the dog to be looked at, so I try to walk quickly. *Just ignore them* is the advice my mother repeatedly gives me, but I've found that silence seems only to make you transparent: it lets them see right through to your weakness. My mother knows about the bullies, the ones who follow me home after primary school, taunting, yelling things at me on the riverbank. She says they're animals.

That's not nice to animals, I say. Recently, aged eleven, I have become a vegetarian. I am always ready to express outrage at any form of animal cruelty or speciesism—my new favorite word, which I have read in *Animal Liberation* by Peter Singer, who is pictured on the cover standing in a field in the dark, looking worried. Speciesism is a word that makes my mother look worried, too, and weary.

The dog skitters on her lead. She hurries ahead, tail between her legs as if suctioned there. I tell her it's all right. She stops, looks back at our accosters, and tries a few high-pitched barks like a seal. I tug on the lead to hurry her on. A dog on a lead is meant to give your walking a purpose, but the only true purpose to our walking is always to turn around and go back home. She wants to go back always, back home. I wish she would run ahead of me, as other dogs do with their owners. Other dogs run ahead, and every so often they'll stop to look back to check that their owner is there, then run on.

The kids are shouting that I'm a snob, and that the dog isn't a dog, but a rat. They shout that they're going to kill the dog.

Something bubbles up in me. "Get fucked," I shout.

The kids explode into laughter. The dog lets out a round of embarrassing barks. "Shut up, you," I say. "This is all your fault." We squelch along the riverbank away from the laughter and toward the bridge. It's autumn; brown and yellow leaves paste the grass.

When we get to the hill, the dog looks up at me forlornly. As always I give in, pick her up, and carry her all the way up Mangarino Road, her wet feet in my hands.

Whenever we go out together, we cause a small scene. People seem to find her incredible. A dog so low to the ground, shaped like a sausage: What's the point of an animal like that? Don't you want a dog shaped like a dog? And I can't remember why, at the beginning, I showed my parents the pictures of miniature dachshunds in my book and insisted that this was the dog for us, for me.

In a book of ghost stories in the school library, I'd read a story about a man named Johnnie Greenwood. Alone at night but for his horse, he had to ride through a wood. As he entered the wood, a black dog appeared. It scampered beside him as he rode. Its eyes were like saucers. When Johnnie emerged from the wood, the dog suddenly vanished. On Johnnie's way home, the dog joined him again, and once clear of the woods, it disappeared again. Years later, it came to light that two men had waited for

Johnnie that night—had planned to murder him in the wood. But the apparition of the black dog frightened them away.

In other stories, phantom black dogs were harbingers of death, sorrow, disease. They had names like Black Shuck, Wild Hunt, and Hellhound. Their eyes beamed red or yellow. And anyone who saw one would probably die. One story tells how some children were bicycling to Hadleigh Castle in Essex when a snarling black dog appeared on their path. Its eyes glowed at them as it bared its teeth. Wailing, the children cycled back home as fast as they could. One by one over the years, they became sick and began to die.

Dogs in stories are always identifiably good dogs or bad dogs. Dogs like Christina's Black Dog are quintessentially good, waiting forever for an absent owner, while the snarling dog near Hadleigh Castle is possessed only by evil.

What confuses me about my dog is that I can't decide whether she's good or bad. I don't know whether the flashes of love that I sometimes feel for her mean that I love her, or just that she is being good in that moment. And, so often, it seems that my mother's love of the dog overshadows mine, so that mine is no longer necessary.

My brothers and I gang up on my mother and the dog. "Why do you let her sleep in the bed? Disgusting."

"It's not disgusting. She's lovely and warm," says Mum. She claims that a little dog is useful as a warm compress for relieving indigestion.

If my father is unhappy about the sleeping arrangements, he keeps quiet. When the dog is in his way he simply picks her up and dumps her on another part of the bed; she bounces and then picks herself up, looking up at him in surprise, this person she loves.

"Be careful," cries my mother. "That's not nice, Russell."

My father is not known for his kindness to animals. He doesn't seem to understand them, what they're for. Once, on a long drive in the South Island, he ran over a turkey and left it, tumbling, on the road behind us. "It was it or us," he said as I screamed. I can never forgive him for the turkey's death. His lack of empathy stings me. Perhaps it is good that my mother is on the dog's side; she can protect her, hold her out of his reach.

In my memory, the dog and my mother are serene together, as if sitting for a portrait, looking out at me. My mother is like a queen, her little lap dog peering out faithfully from under her arm.

One night, when my mother and the dog come to say good night, I turn on her accusingly: "You care about the dog more than me." I've been holding on to this line for a long time, waiting for my moment. Now that I've said it, my throat clamps up.

My mother protests that this isn't true. She's laughing a little.

"Yes, it is. That's what it feels like." I'm standing at the window beside my bed, and now I press my face against it. The lights outside are streaming.

I can tell that my mother's hands are on her hips. "Stop this nonsense. You've got a whole new day tomorrow. Isn't that good? You don't have to do a thing, and God will hand you a brand-new day on a plate."

Or am I putting words into her mouth? Often she talked about how lucky we were to have hundreds of chances, one after the other, to be better—each chance a new life coming with the day. Push open the curtains and there it is in the sky above our town. But I don't know for sure if she reminded me of this when I accused her of caring more about the dog than me. I do remember that she went away, leaving the dog this time, and I hugged the dog and she licked my face. Things were better between us when one of us was upset. For instance, once when she got a bone stuck in her tooth, I had to tug it out of her mouth with pliers as she squirmed and grumbled, and afterward we lay down together on the front porch, exhausted, her head in my lap. I liked to think she was grateful for a little while, that she knew I had saved her.

The dog has developed an odd tremor in her neck. Her head arches to one side as if she's listening for something. After some weeks of this, her tremoring becomes more urgent, as if her head is being pulled sideways. She gets a glazed look in her eye. My mother is irritated at first and tells her to stop it. But the dog keeps trembling; even her eyes seem to tremble, the water in them too.

She begins waiting at the bottom of steps. She wants to be

picked up. "Lazy," we say. But something is wrong. She is beginning to drag her back legs behind her. She won't walk with me at all anymore. It's less hassle just to carry her, and even then she squirms, wanting down, her front feet kicking while her back legs dangle.

At night Mum bundles her in a tartan rug and carries her out to the trailer, a quiet place where she can study her Japanese. They sit together at the little table, which can also be folded out into a bed. The dog can't hop up and down the steps anymore. Mum is always there, the dog's personal chairlift.

"She shouldn't be sleeping in the bed now," I say, when they visit me to say good night. "What if it makes her worse?"

Mum holds the dog to her chest. "She'll be all right. Won't you, darling." The dog's head quivers and quivers.

The vet is a cheerful man who is always telling a joke and letting out loud guffaws. He is as tall as it is possible to be. As he and my mother and I stand around the examination table, he strokes the dog, pushing her down with his strong brown hands as if trying to stroke the fear out of her. For a moment she stops trembling and looks up at us and moves her tail. "A good sign," says the vet. His eyes are kind.

The dog has a disease to do with the discs in her spine. For the vet to see what is going on she would need to have a special dye injected into her spine, so that it shows up in an X-ray. And after that she could have an operation. Back problems are common in dachshunds: running up and down steps, leaping up and down from laps and beds—we shouldn't be surprised, the vet says. The operation will cost thousands of dollars.

He gives us a large metal crate to keep her in. "Keep her in there for now. She shouldn't be moving around."

The crate goes in the kitchen. I put some cushions and the tartan rug inside, then put the dog on top. She flops to one side. I can't bring myself to shut the door of the crate. Why haven't I been nicer to her? Why did I stop wanting her?

"Black dog. You'll be all right." I stroke her head, trying to soothe its shivering, then I shut the door.

Maybe I have grown bored with her, the way she never comes when you call her, the fleas on her belly, the way she gets under the house and barks at hedgehogs, the things she drags into the hallway. Early in the morning I'd hear the snuffling sounds, and when I opened my bedroom door her eyes would shine out of the dark; she'd be hunkered over something bloody and dirty. The growls that came out of her when I tried to take it off her were the growls of a big dog. She has never bitten me—at least, not with intent—but in those moments I know she could. In her body, low to the ground, there is an animal.

Even fully grown, she is much smaller than the cat. The cat is an elderly black-and-white stalker with a swinging belly, but her paws are quick and she is more agile than the dog. The fights are explosive. The cat scratches the dog's nose and the dog screams; then, muttering, the dog turns around and backs the cat into a corner with her rear end. She waggles her bottom and looks over her shoulder, grinning, until the cat slips past like an eel, disgusted. She stalks into a corner and begins cleaning herself furiously. The fights never progress much past this. The cat barely tolerates the dog and the dog delights in putting the cat in undignified situations after which she must clean herself.

We grew up together, the cat and me. She came to live with the family just a few days after I did. Maybe the cat is more mine than the dog. Maybe the dog and I have become a chore to each other—the walks, the baths, the fleas, the bones, and now the trembling, the crate, things to be worried over.

In the crate she wheezes silently with her mouth wide open and her head arched to one side. Other times she wriggles around on the floor in circles, and at horrible moments it looks as though she's dancing. I crouch behind the cage to make the soothing, kissing noises we've always made, but it's as though she doesn't hear. She seems to cower as she stares at me. I wonder what she sees, if it's still me. In the evenings, we take her out of the cage and lay her on the couch while my parents watch *Coronation Street*, and the whole time she keeps up her whimpering and muttering, a kind of song.

After school I ask my mother, "What are we going to do?" My mother's face creases; she stands in the kitchen with one hand on her hip and the other over her mouth.

I don't know if this is a true memory, but on another afternoon my mother comes home cradling the cane basket in both arms, and the dog curled inside, sleeping.

Years later, as a university student, I have a job walking a German shepherd, Tāne. Tāne belongs to a wealthy man. He and I set out each day around the bay and up steep hills. He's lunging and unpredictable, and the first time I let him off his lead he tears into the trees and returns covered in filth, happy. The next day he's clean and brushed, smelling of geraniums. When I'm not there, he spends all day by himself in the man's apartment.

Sometimes when we're walking through the bush, when it's winter, early afternoon, when the air is quiet under the branches and it's just the pair of us, and the sound of his breathing is like something being folded and refolded, I imagine that he's my dog and that, instead of walking back to the spacious air-conditioned apartment with its massive bookshelves and its gleaming kitchen with many different beautiful knives, we're walking home to my student flat in Aro Valley.

There are many dogs in the city. A fat Labrador bobbling along behind its owner in Newtown; two stately black-and-tan dachshunds trotting competently beside a man in a bowler hat; a black dog, whose breed I don't know, skittering down Vivian Street, seemingly without owner.

Whenever I see a dog I want to kneel down and get its face between my hands and look into its eyes. I can imagine that I see my dog's eyes there. It is like opening a book.

In this book there is a picture of my dog in her cane basket. She is wrapped in her tartan blanket, her head tucked under like a swan's. She's curled up, perfectly asleep. I touch her but she's cold and hard, as if she has set. I realize that my mother made the decision alone. I sit on the porch beside the dog. She is wrapped as neatly as a gift.

But in the book, too, my brother and I crouch in the hallway and roll a tennis ball between us. We are chanting. "Black dog, black dog!" She gallops up and down, ears flying, and is a pup again.

In my memory the hallway is dark, like a wood, and sometimes we run through it together. She protects me.

katherine would approve

On Katherine Mansfield's birthday I walked up the edge of a long driveway in gale-force winds. I walked for a long time, with cars passing me. *The wind—the wind.* I was walking to Government House, which was at the top of the hill, where there would be a party. Katherine Mansfield was 125 years old today. The driveway to Government House has bushes and trees on either side, and these were beaten and pushed about by the wind. I thought about turning around and just going home, but that would mean walking past the guard at the entrance again. Every time someone drove past me I felt more self-conscious. Finally a hybrid car stopped and a woman wound down the window. "Are you going to the Katherine Mansfield party?" I was. "That's a long way, dear. Do you want to hop in?" As we zoomed up the hill between the trees, we should've talked about the end of Mansfield's story "The Garden Party," where a big dog runs by like a shadow and Laura walks down that smoky dark lane, because that driveway recalled it to us. But instead we talked about whether we'd been to Government House before. The woman had been many times. I hadn't been.

Government House, the governor-general's official residence, is an enormous brown-and-cream building with dark jarrah weatherboards and a flag tower. A rectangular pond is feathered by the wind. Cars were still creeping over the pristine gravel or were parked nearby, and the new director of the Katherine Mansfield Birthplace, a woman named Emma, was standing by the door with one of the board members, greeting people. I'd met Emma at the Birthplace that morning, my final morning as the acting director. I'd shown her through the house: the tiny office stacked high with filing boxes, where the new director would sit each day; the scullery with its steel pots hung on the walls and its meat grinder, on which she too would bruise her leg as she went by; the dim, roped-off bedroom where Mansfield was born, where a hairbrush and hand mirror were fixed with catgut to a dressing table, and where a dehumidifier now hummed and slurped. At the end of every day, the birthroom dehumidifier was heavy with water. Now Emma would be the one to carry the bucket down the stairs and empty it in the little sink in the scullery. I'd handed her my lump of keys, which opened countless cupboards and cabinets and internal doors, then wheeled my bike out from where I'd parked it behind a sack of blood-and-bone in the rose garden and cycled down Tinakori Road, grinning as the wind pushed me on.

I got the job at the Birthplace on a whim. The previous director had left suddenly, and the board needed someone to look after the volunteers, to schedule tours, and to organize that year's birthday party while a new permanent director was found. I'd visited the house—a square weatherboard building with a red corrugated-iron roof, built in 1887—on a school trip when I was maybe nine or ten, and I knew that Mansfield, a famous writer whose story about a garden party had frightened me, had lived there until she was five years old. But I couldn't remember much beyond heavy Victorian furniture and dark drapes, and walls lined with photographs of Katherine and her family.

On my first morning I sat nervously in the cold kitchen. It was my first full-time job in a long time. The chairman of the Katherine Mansfield Birthplace Society and the four paid staff were there, all in winter coats. "Ashleigh will be here five days a week," the chairman told us all firmly, "and she'll be in charge. She is our director for the foreseeable future." The kitchen had stained timber walls and a hefty coal range. Pretty floral plates were held in place with wire on a sideboard. A bowl of Granny Smith apples was set on a velvet tablecloth below a single window that overlooked the back garden. I later learned that the garden had once sloped into a gully. Mansfield had complained about wretched people throwing their empty cans into it. And also in the kitchen was the replica of Mansfield's doll's house, painted spinach green with yellow windowpanes and a red roof. Its frontage was locked but two figures collapsed in armchairs were visible through a window. *Open it, quickly, someone!* I knew that inside, the rooms would be papered, and that in the middle of the dining room table would be a tiny amber lamp.

Greg introduced me to Caryl, who managed the accounts, a pretty-faced, silver-haired woman with red lipstick; to Linda, whose current job was to sort all the files in the upstairs office (once a nursery) and who had a bad back and seemed to communicate mainly in rapid eye blinks and hand gestures; and to Sue, who worked only on Sundays but had made a special trip to meet me today. "It's wonderful to have you here," she said with glistening eyes, "in the grotto." I'd passed her a few minutes before, as I pushed my bike on the footpath toward the house, and she had beamed at me. "I knew it must've been you," she said now. "You had Katherine's look about you." Sue was in her sixties, with bright gold hair and a constant smile. Over the coming weeks, every Monday I would find long, barely readable notes written on scraps of paper and folded into the appointment book. "Ash babe," Sue wrote (or sometimes "wonder bunny," a name she'd designated seemingly at random), "a very quiet day in the grotto today." Then there was Daniel, who introduced himself as "the education curator" and stared past my face when he shook my hand. He had one brown eye and one blue eye. He looked at my brooch, which was shaped like a blossom. "Nice *brooch*. Katherine would approve," he said. "You know she called her brooch 'the little eye.'" I would soon learn that Daniel talked about Mansfield as if he had known her, personally, as a friend.

When the chairman left us and the day got under way, Daniel instructed me to cut the scones he had baked for some visitors from a retirement village, who were coming for "Victorian high tea." The scones, hard and dry, disintegrated as I cut them, and when Daniel saw what had happened he cried out, "Look. What an *absolute* mess. I don't think Katherine would be happy." My scone mishap was the beginning of a fraught working relationship whereby I would try to please Daniel, and would feel pleased when he confided in me, usually about the flaws of the other staff, or about his regrets from his former teaching career. I felt calm when he was happy and tense when he was flustered. "Oh, Katherine," he would say, when one of the volunteer gardeners brought in a posy of cinerarias or marigolds. "Katherine loved these flowers." Whenever a group of students touring the house didn't pay attention to his lecturing, or tried to sneak into roped-off areas of the house, he would shout, "Katherine wouldn't approve of that."

I came to learn that Daniel was one of many people who wielded a strong view of what Mansfield was like as a person. There was a particular set of statements the volunteer tour guides would repeat, and that visitors would say back to them; these were deep within the narrative of the house. "She was ahead of her time." "A radical in many ways." "Very stylish." "A truly modern woman who cast off convention." And sometimes, conspiratorially, "She was very likely a lesbian." Sometimes visitors would talk about her life with admiration, and then confess to me as they left the house, "I've never actually read any of her stuff. I should." The tour guides who had led groups through the house for decades seemed to believe that Mansfield's childhood home was the most important part, the most telling part, of her life. Maybe it was, because it was tangible. You could step inside and imagine yourself to be a child in another century. You could detect echoes of this house in some of Mansfield's stories—the deep tangled gully seen from a window in "The Aloe"; a fireplace choked with rubbish in "Prelude"—and recognizing these echoes felt like knowing her.

There were also visitors who didn't know where they were, or who Katherine Mansfield was. These were mostly young schoolchildren, but one afternoon a group from Alzheimers Wellington arrived. About twenty elderly men and women drifted slowly into the house, with canes and walkers, their minder following. "Are you her?" a woman asked me, pointing at a poster of Mansfield on the wall. "You have her hair." I laughed and tried to explain, but the woman was wandering away. "It's not as nice as my house," someone else said. "This isn't my house," another woman snapped. None of the group could climb the stairs to see the room where Mansfield was born, so the volunteer tour guide and I ushered them into the garden, and the group began to drift slowly and silently apart, all of them with their heads down, looking at their feet on the lawn. And after a few minutes of this, their minder from Alzheimers Wellington had them return to the van and they drove away. I went back inside to the tiny office and thought how their childhoods were the closest in time to Mansfield's childhood, but in every other way they were so far away from her, she was invisible.

. . .

I learned a lot about the house from Daniel, because he led the most tours. His voice twanged through the building, often on the verge of a shout or, it seemed, a sob. I learned that the chinoiserie-patterned wallpaper in the stairwell featured the ancient symbol for good luck that was later appropriated by the Nazis, and that visitors often complained about it. That in an archaeological dig around the house men had found tea-set fragments, marbles, a white ceramic mouse, and pieces of a comb. That the grim-looking fruitcake on the dining table had been baked many years ago and then painted with resin—"No, it *wouldn't* taste nice," Daniel told children sharply. That the stuffed birds in display cases "reflected a Victorian preoccupation with collecting." That none of the furniture was original except for the three spindly chairs around a table in the drawing room, and the sagging wooden bench in the kitchen, where I once spilled a full pot of coffee. And that until she was five, Mansfield had lived here with her parents Harold and Annie Beauchamp; her sisters Vera, Charlotte, and Jeanne; her two teenage aunts, Belle and Kitty; and her grandmother Margaret. There was another daughter, too—Gwendoline, who died from infantile cholera. In the dining room, where another dehumidifier droned, there was a photo of Granny Dyer holding the dead baby Gwendoline, who was dressed to look as if she were alive. Her mouth was ajar, as if sleepily. Postmortem photography wasn't unusual in the late 1800s—deceased people would be dressed and positioned as if posing steadily for the camera—but I could never bring myself to look at that picture for long, Granny Dyer watching so tenderly over her granddaughter. Later the Beau-champs had a son, too, when they moved to another house. Leslie was killed in World War I when a grenade he was holding in his hand accidentally exploded.

The Birthplace existed in a space between exhilaration—some people were visibly excited, humbled, when they walked through their hero's childhood home—and a deep stagnation that you could feel when you walked through the rooms alone at the end of the day. The air felt stale, as if it too were preserved in resin. It was important to unplug all electrical appliances at day's end, because the volunteers, the staff, and the board all shared a great fear of electrical fire. "Gosh, I've had nightmares about it," Sue told me, "just *imagine*," and she put her hands over her mouth. It was as if fire were inevitable, just like "the big one," Wellington's devastating earthquake of a future century. The fear infected me too. In my first weeks, when I did my late afternoon rounds, unplugging lamps and heaters, crawling on hands and knees to reach sockets, my hands would tremble. And I did imagine. I imagined wheeling my bike up the driveway one morning, the house a charred shell before me, the dolls, the birds, the pretty plates just lumps in the ash. I would have to phone the chairman. "Greg. I'm so sorry." But part of me believed that fire just wasn't possible. The air in the house wouldn't carry fire.

I was in the office when an earthquake of 6.6 magnitude struck one Friday in August. Until that moment there had been a profound quietness inside the house, except, as always, for one sound—a branch, outside the office, making a high-pitched fluting sound as it brushed against the window. It was the most mournful sound, and I couldn't help but imagine that Mansfield had heard it herself. The office, about the size of a linen cupboard and stacked high with yellowing boxes and ring binders, had once been a bathroom; Mansfield had bathed in here as a child.

When the quake hit, the office swerved side to side, as if the house were trying to swim. Upstairs, I heard Daniel shouting. I ducked under the tiny desk and held my breath, while the house continued its strange, static shuffling. I could hear the staircase squeaking, as if hundreds of feet were going up and down all at once. Later, when I thought about that sound, I remembered that Mansfield had died shortly after running up a flight of stairs, perhaps to prove how well she was.

"It's not at all surprising, given it's survived since the 1880s," said the chairman on the phone. He said it was probably the safest house in Wellington because it was all wood, and wood moved flexibly with the earth. The only thing that happened during the earthquake was that a photo of Mansfield as a young woman fell off a wall upstairs, but was undamaged.

Inside Government House there were chandeliers and a huge gilt-framed portrait of Queen Elizabeth at the head of the ballroom. The room was filled with people. Lawyers, museum curators, and politicians—members of parliament, councilors, ambassadors of all the countries Mansfield had visited.

"Twenty-five years ago today," the governor-general said, reading from his notes, "Lady Beverley Reeves officially opened the restored Beauchamp family home at 25 Tinakori Road. The realization that the house where Mansfield was born still stood was the heritage equivalent of finding one of her unpublished short stories in an attic!" There was a roar of laughter. The governor-general spoke of how the restoration of the house brought Mansfield back to her own country, and of how desperate she was to escape "the socially rigid life of Wellington, which she considered no match for the bohemian joys and intellectual delights she thought she'd find in London." He spoke of how her character was shaped by New Zealand. Finally, he said, "I have to admit I haven't actually read any Katherine Mansfield."

At first there was laughter, but then I felt around me some ripples of consternation, of disbelief. Someone quavered, "How awful." And you could sense the governor-general realizing what he had done, and that he shouldn't have told the truth. He tried to save himself by raising his hands and chuckling.

"But, but, Katherine Mansfield has always been so"—he paused for a while, seeming to struggle—"*big*. She's always been at the forefront of our literary consciousness. When I was growing up there was always a sense of how—*big*—she was." He turned back to his notes, and was emboldened. "She helped to revolutionize the English short story, and left behind a body of work that is as sharp, intriguing, and fresh as the day it was written."

Before I left the party I said good-bye to the volunteer gardeners, who were standing together drinking from wineglasses and eating egg sandwiches. I'd never seen them in formal clothes, instead of grubby pants and gloves. I liked the gardeners. They came every week, with their clippers and trowels, to rigorously tend the plants that were mentioned in Mansfield's stories and letters: cinerarias, arum lilies, pot marigolds, and the mignonette around the front doorway, whose perfume had been "recalled by a visitor" in the early 1900s.

I walked all the way back down the driveway, which was darkening now. *The wind—the wind.* I felt enormously relieved to be free. I berated myself, as I had so many times over the past months at the Birthplace: I should've treasured this experience. I should have let it soak into me freely and without complaint. I should have risen above even Mansfield herself! "Horrid little piggy house," she'd said about the place, remembering it much later, from London. Well, I would miss having a place to go each day, instead of working in the little study at my suburban flat, but that was all I would miss: a place to go. And that, it seemed to me, was disrespectful, even shameful. "What a fantastic job for a writer," people had said to me, "to sit in Katherine Mansfield's house all day." And I'd agreed. It was. I didn't say that I was the wrong writer to be sitting in it.

Perhaps worse, though, was that I no longer loved Mansfield's stories as I had before. Having heard the tour guides reference them over and over—there was Daniel, shouting, as he pointed at the doll's house, "And if you look inside, you will see the little lamp!"—the stories seemed not to belong to me now. People had crowded inside them and were digging between words for something new to hold up and turn in the light. I couldn't hold them close to me without feeling someone looking over my shoulder. Without noticing the empty cans thrown in the gully.

It was the end of the school day, and at the bottom of the driveway I got caught in a stream of students leaving their school gates. A group of boys were shouting at one another about how far through an Xbox game they were, and how one of their teachers in particular was a dickhead and they couldn't wait to leave, they just couldn't wait to get out.

wolf man

The thing that interested me wasn't the fact that she had facial hair. It was the fact that everyone can be amazed by it, everyone can be thinking about it, everyone can see it as an interesting thing, but no one can say anything.

—Media commentator Paul Henry on Greenpeace activist Stephanie Mills's moustache, March 2009

My father wouldn't look at my face. He looked into the space above my head, or at one of my ears, or he'd close his eyes. This time though, after we hugged good-bye—our brief, angular hug—he looked right at me.

"You've got a little moustache," he said, "just like I used to have."

His voice was thoughtful, as if he were saying, "I seem to remember they had that dog that barked all hours of the night," or "I suppose there are some terrible collisions on these roads."

We stood beside the waiting taxi. My parents had flown down for the weekend to see the hostel where I was staying for my first year at university. Before I could say anything, my mother was talking again. She would not pause until they were both bundled into the taxi. Then they were off.

I kept my head down as I walked toward the cable car. My face was very heavy. It was only inside the car, empty except for an elderly couple, that I put a finger to my upper lip.

I had always known it was there, but knowing and acknowledging are different things. Until now I had managed to avoid looking at it directly. Like my father I found it easier to look at the edges of things.

In my hostel room I looked at the mirror. I tried to see myself through my father's eyes. My face is mostly eyes. Thick eyebrows, eyelashes that frequently impale the corners of my eyes, a nose already becoming hooklike, like my father's. And then, there it was. The little moustache. Faint, but faint was already a mistake. Faint was more than enough to draw the eye, in the way that faint lines on a weather map tell us what's to come. I drew a finger over it and saw that the hair was plentiful enough to move sideways. A moustache must be all or nothing. Dark and bristling, accompanied by a flushed face and small suspicious eyes, like *Father Ted*'s Mrs. Doyle, or not there at all: the skin bare, innocent of transgression, like a model in *Vogue* whose skin barely seems made, a shining bubble she will occupy for only a second.

As I studied my moustache, I thought about why it was that my father's observation had made it this far with me—all the way down Lambton Quay, up the hill via cable car, through the playground, into my room—because it was really no different from the kinds of things he would usually say. It was his way to drop incongruous statements into the middle of long silences and no one could ever be prepared. "That boyfriend of yours seems a bit glum." "Those trousers look like something out of *Ghostbusters*." "That music is hideous." He would follow these statements with more silence, leaving you upended. Most of the remarks were easy to brush away; since neither of us would meet the other's eye, I could pretend he was confused, that he didn't know what he was talking about. Yet somehow that old rebuff— *You don't know anything about me*—couldn't carry the weight for me this time. This time he knew exactly what he was talking about. The moustache could not be denied.

The truth was, I already had a preoccupation with body hair. It had begun early. I was aware of hair, because compared with other girls, even some boys, I was very obviously hairy. I had hairy arms, especially. "You're a wee monkey," said my mother, with affection in her voice. I didn't mind being her monkey. It was when a boy in my class saw my arms and called me Wolf Man that my feelings about hairiness changed. In the 1941 film *The Wolf Man*, the eponymous monster is an oddly sheep-like werewolf, with bristly facial fur and a mostly sheepish expression. I didn't want to be a monster. I didn't want to be a wolf. Most of all, I didn't want to be a man.

After that, whenever it was too hot to wear a jumper, I tried to hide my arms. But at school it always seemed to be too hot. The rugby field was parched and prickly. Wet swimsuits and towels heated up in the plastic bags we carried back from the pool. The asphalt was scorching; the Mangaokewa River was flattened by the heat. When sitting, I folded my arms behind me, tried to sit on them, twisted them so that only the undersides, the less hairy parts, could be seen. I wonder now if this is the reason why today I can bend my arms at horrible angles. Self-consciousness can make people contort themselves in incredible ways. The contortions become more than habits; they grow into us, become us.

"Why don't you shave your arms?" my friend suggested. "Then you wouldn't look like such a freak." That seemed an easy way to untangle myself, so one afternoon I did. Sheaves of blond hair clogged the basin, my mother's leg razor overcome. My arms slowly emerged. They were weirdly soft, as if newborn. I blotted them dry and stretched them out in front of me. I hardly believed that they were mine.

For a few days I loved my new arms. I studied the moles, elevated after so long undercover. I loved being able to feel towels, sheets, and polar fleece on my skin. This was how a girl's arms should be, as long and smooth as pieces of bamboo. But only a few days passed before a dark wave of stubble began to rise.

"Your arms are prickling me," another of my friends complained. "It's like you've got thorns." We were sitting together on the wall between our school and the road. In the hollows of the wall on either side of us, there was a garden filled with pink, red, and yellow roses. Often we buried our faces in the petals. It was almost too much, the smell of school roses; they were more potent than the roses that grew in our garden at home. When we got tired of smelling the school roses, we played Rhinoceros, snapping off the thorns and sticking them onto our noses. As far as I could see, thorns had only one purpose and that was Rhinoceros, the game where the person with the most thorns won.

As soon as I could, I took to my arms again with the razor. But a few days later the same thing happened. First the ominous prickling, then the hair coming out like barbs. I knew now that there was no escape; I would have to give myself over to my fate. I left the hair to grow, which it did, and it seemed more wolf-like than before.

Each time we visited Hamilton, I went to a bookshop to riffle through a box of postcards on the counter. For $1.50 each I would buy the most mysterious postcards I could find so that I could add them to the lattice of pictures on my bedroom wall. It was in the box that I found a self-portrait of Frida Kahlo.

I placed Frida's picture between the picture of the red girl in the mirror and the flying woman tugging on the hand of her earthbound husband. I took a long time to bring myself to closely study the self-portrait. It was because of her moustache; I was a little afraid of it. It made her into a double-sided optical illusion, like the image of the old woman and the young woman concealed inside each other. But once I saw that she was beautiful I couldn't see anything else. The moustache was not only incidental but a mark of her strength and conviction. It couldn't have been any other way. It was like the crumbled-away shoulder of the Venus de Milo.

There must be other women, ordinary women, who had moustaches and body hair but who were also beautiful—even if they lived in the depths of strangeness, even if to so many of us they were more frightening than alluring. Didn't that just mean that their beauty came from a different place, that to find it you needed to learn a different way of looking? Perhaps it was only in the future that the way would be found. Somewhere, I'd read a quote by Francis Bacon: "There is no excellent beauty that hath not some strangeness in the proportion." I had no idea who Bacon was, but I decided this was true. The question seemed to be how much strangeness our eyes would allow before the balance tipped too far.

If I had liked confrontation, I would have shown my father the portrait of Frida Kahlo. "Look, she's got a moustache," I'd say, "and you have to admit, Dad, she's beautiful." But I don't think he would have agreed. The only person I remember him describing as beautiful was Michelle Phillips, the singer in the Mamas and the Papas. It was on Christmas Day. We were sitting on the living room floor as "Twelve Thirty (Young Girls Are Coming to the Canyon)" played on the dusty speakers. My father was staring at Michelle Phillips's picture inside the CD booklet. She had long golden hair with a center part, and a perfect elfin face. "She is the most beautiful woman in the world," my father suddenly said. His voice moved up the register as it always did when he was insisting on the truth.

I didn't like that he had said "beautiful"—in his mouth it was embarrassing, it was explicit. But at the same time I was taken aback, I was impressed, that he saw beauty and then said so.

There is a description of a woman named Barbara Urselin, known as the Hairy Maid, in the diary of the seventeenth-century English writer John Evelyn. Barbara almost certainly had hypertrichosis, a rare condition of excessive hairiness, sometimes known as human werewolf syndrome. From an early age in the 1630s, Barbara had been paraded around Europe as a freak. Evelyn recounts how

> her very Eyebrowes were combed upward, & all her forehead as thick & even as growes on any womans head, neately dress'd: There comes also tw[o] lock[s] very long out of Each Eare: she had also a most prolix beard, & mustachios, with long lockes of haire growing on the very middle of her nose, exactly like an Island Dog: the rest of her body not so hairy, yet exceedingly long in comparison, armes, neck, breast & back; the [Colour] of a bright browne, & fine as well dressed flax.

What strikes me about this description is its gentleness. To Evelyn, Barbara's appearance is not monstrous or even ugly. Behind all that hair is a civilizing influence that sees the flaxen hair carefully combed and smoothed. Barbara has "locks," not the fur of a wolf, and the hairiness seems to grow with design: a lock grows out of each ear; the hair appears "on the very middle of her nose, exactly like an Island Dog." Barbara is unusually hairy, but she is still a lady. By writing about her in this way, Evelyn transforms her condition into something that might be beautiful.

You could compare Evelyn's description with one that appeared two hundred years later of Julia Pastrana, another human werewolf who, like Barbara, featured in her very own freak show. In 1854, Julia was exhibited in New York at the Gothic Hall on

Broadway as "The Marvelous Hybrid or Bear Woman," with a promotional flyer for the show proclaiming that "its jaws, jagged fangs and ears are terrifically hideous . . . Nearly its whole frame is coated with long glossy hair . . . this semi-human being is perfectly docile, and speaks the Spanish language." According to this description, Julia was not human. But in her famous photograph she wears a lovely dress covered in flowers. Her stance is masculine, with hands placed casually on her hips, feet far apart; her shoes are pointy winklepickers. Her lips protrude as she gazes nonchalantly to one side, like a bored cowboy. Her mass of hair is pulled back off her face and pinned with what looks like flowers. She wears a string of pearls. These are all the trappings of a beautiful human woman—but there she is with that tremendous beard, ruining it all.

Julia Pastrana was a show woman. She could sing—the newspapers praised her "harmonious voice"—and during her exhibition she sang romantic songs in both Spanish and English. She could also dance: she waltzed with soldiers at military galas and performed elaborate Spanish dances on stage. Far from humanizing her, these performances must have made her that much more a spectacle: Hear the ape sing! See it dance! Her talents did little to persuade her audience that she was a human being, much less a woman. In the late 1850s her "handler" married her—and we can assume that he did so only to claim legal ownership of his exhibit, because after Julia died in 1860 during childbirth, her husband had her mummified, along with her hairy stillborn child. The pair was placed in an anatomical museum, Julia dressed in a colorful dancing costume and her son in a sailor's suit.

You can buy a hand-embroidered doll of Julia. An artist has set up an online store that specializes in dolls of traveling freak show exhibits. The Julia doll is made from leather with little hairs painstakingly sewed into it "for a more realistically hairy effect." It wears a Russian dance costume of soft yellow fabric.

My moustache was negligible in comparison to the hair on the faces of these women. But I think my response to my moustache, and maybe also my father's response to my moustache, came from the same well of fear and fascination that once insisted that a woman like Julia Pastrana belonged in a freak show. Maybe it is the same fear that others have too. You can see it in the great variety of ways that a woman may get rid of her moustache, of all of her unwanted hair. She can dissolve the hair with a special cream; pull it out by its roots with a pair of tweezers or with hot wax; deaden it with a laser; electrocute it with a metal probe; have it plucked out, hair by hair, with a quick-moving thread; with a mechanized device she can rapidly grasp and extract the moustache; with chemical bleach she can create the illusion of soft, fair hair; she can shave it off; she can slough it away with sandpaper; she can smother it in a paste of turmeric and rock salt each day. Our discomfort with hair has moved underground. Many of us now simply accept that the hair cannot stay. The discomfort seems to grow from within, as if it had its own dermis, epidermis, follicles.

Like me, my mother had a moustache. Not dramatic, but noticeable. She, too, decided to banish it with a razor. Of course, she was doomed to repeat the task forevermore, often leaving the hair to grow bristly for weeks at a time. When she kissed me, I could feel the soft prickle of her upper lip, like a man's. My father never mentioned it. But I did, once or twice. I felt an urgency to tell her.

"You shouldn't shave your upper lip," I told her sternly.

She put a hand over her mouth. "Oh, dear. Does it look terrible?"

I just grimaced. My cruel work was done. Even if she didn't do something about it, at least now she knew. There was power in knowing. Then you could make the call yourself over what you wanted the world to see.

Whether moustacheless or mustachioed, my mother never succeeded in getting my father to say she was beautiful. He was the first to call her "Toad," the pet name that eventually became her family nickname, an ill-fitting one because she was not like a toad at all—she towered over all of us, was lean and strident, she wore polka-dotted skirts and bright velvet blouses. Sometimes she asked me to give her a "facial" and I would push an elastic headband into her hair and rub creams into her face, wiping them off with a facecloth that I dipped into a baking bowl full of warm water. I would study her face while her eyes were closed, and with her hair pushed back, her skin damp, her face lost its sternness and looked almost girlish. Later, dressed up to go out, she would say, "Doesn't Toad look beautiful?" Standing in the kitchen, with her coral-colored lipstick on, she would put her hands on her hips and push out her bust. My father would give a soft laugh as he bent to tie his shoelaces or reached up to smooth his hair.

In another story I shrug off my father's comment. Like a proud, eccentric man I grow my moustache long so that I can gel it into spikes and twist it into curls. I walk down the street wearing winklepickers and a top hat; maybe I carry a cane and have a little dachshund on a lead; I wear a faint smile under my moustache.

I am like Jennifer Miller, one of the famous modern-day bearded ladies, a circus performer who juggles clubs with muscular arms and wrestles herself out of straitjackets. "This act has been done for centuries," she cries. "It means something to people: it means freedom!" And she breaks free. In photos, her beard flows over the edge of her pretty face. "Hair is a symbol of power," she says. "So, here I am, a gal with a beard, prancing around the streets of New York."

I have the calm demeanor of the little girl Tognina in a portrait by the Bolognese painter Lavinia Fontana. The girl has dark eyes and rosy lips and her face is covered in hair. She looks soft, like a cat. Her dark eyes, rimmed with pink, gaze calmly out of all that hair. Tognina belonged to a family who all, except their mother, had thick, dark facial hair, and later she bore several hairy children herself.

I once saw an exhibition of mustachioed and bearded women. The canvases were huge. Some women wore lipstick and eyeliner; on these women the facial hair looked like just another frill or ornament, like a piercing. Other women had gone out of their way to look masculine, with white shirts buttoned to the neck, buzzed haircuts, and no makeup. There is no doubt that all of the women were deeply interesting. They had brave, compelling faces. They looked their audience straight in the eyes. "Ask me anything," their faces seemed to say, "and I can tell you."

I looked hard at them. I closed my eyes and opened them quickly to surprise myself. I couldn't see beauty—not yet. If they were beautiful now, their faces wouldn't have filled the art gallery so that people could stare and be challenged to decide: beautiful or ugly? Maybe, in another story, I would answer with conviction worthy of Frida Kahlo's moustache, worthy of Julia Pastrana's song "Beautiful."

In this story, however, I couldn't sleep after saying good-bye to my parents. Again I saw my father studying my face as if seeing me for the first time. That was the last picture he had of me: a girl with a moustache, speechless. Again I saw the taxi driving away. I needed to defend myself, but what could I say out loud? I had an argument, but it belonged in a first-year essay. "In itself, hair is meaningless," the essay began. "It is only our way of seeing that makes it socially unacceptable." I curled into a ball in my bed, alternately reciting my argument and berating myself for caring what my father said.

If the bearded lady Jennifer Miller could see me now, she would put her strong, veined hands on my shoulders and give me a shake. "Listen to me. Hair is power! That's why men don't want women to have too much of it."

As we faced each other in bed the day after my parents' visit, my boyfriend suddenly reached out and touched my upper lip.

"What happened?"

I turned away. "Nothing."

I heard a smile in his voice. "Did you get rid of your moustache?"

"What? No! What moustache?"

"You did get rid of it. It's not there anymore."

I turned back. "All right. I did. Does it look terrible?"

He squinted. "It looks . . . bare."

He was right. Deforested, the skin looked unnaturally bare.

I had waxed it off, and my face looked smaller and paler, as if I'd been down a well for a few days. But it was also, I felt, the face that everyone should have seen all along.

"Does it look bad?" I asked again. I waited for him to say it didn't. This was how it worked between us. I would talk about how ugly I felt, and he would be upset. Over and over again, he would tell me I was beautiful. "I'm going to keep saying it until you believe it. I don't care if it takes ninety years." He'd say, "Even if you weighed three hundred kilograms I would still think you were the most beautiful woman in the world." He'd say, "Why don't you believe me?" The next day we would do it all over again. It was true, I didn't believe him, but I couldn't get enough of being told. It was as if I gorged on the words, stuffing myself full. Later, in private, I purged myself of them.

He squinted at my face again. "It does look kind of weird. There's something missing, but it takes a while to figure out what it is," he went on. "You know? You're still you, but there's an absence."

There's an old photograph of my father and me together—me at seven with a heavy fringe, Dad in his thirties with his glossy black hair and V-shaped pilot's moustache. (As a recreational pilot, my father does not wear a uniform—his flying garb is polo shirt, beige shorts, Velcro sandals.) While he chuckles about something, I'm peering off to the side, distinctly glum.

Glum seemed to be one of his favorite words; I remember him using it with me often as I lolled mournfully on a chair or pulled a duvet around my head in my parents' huge flannelly bed. "You're looking a bit *glum*." When I didn't respond he would pucker his chin, look troubled, and say nothing else.

The next time I saw him after the weekend in Wellington, I watched his face closely. I wanted him to see my new face, the one he should have seen all along. I made sure I stayed in his line of view, and I checked his expression now and then. I am still waiting for him to say something.

she cannot work

She cannot work when the man is in the house. She is working on a project that she has been working on for a long time, and ever since she began living with the man the project has been moving slowly and she is no longer sure that she will finish it. In the evenings, after they watch the TV show they both like, she and the man lie on the couch together reading or looking at their computers, and sometimes she will try, secretly, to work on her project, but, after a few minutes, the man will hear her hesitant typing and look up from his book to ask her what she is doing. She can't tell him about the project, because once, when she felt tired of his questions about it, she told him she had stopped working on it. Too many things had changed since she began all those years ago, she said, so it no longer made sense to continue, and instead she would spend her spare time on her studies. But the truth is that she has continued. All this time, she has continued, even though it is true, she supposes, that it does not make sense to continue.

Every week she looks forward to Sunday afternoon because that is when the man will go for a long ride on his bicycle. She will have the house to herself then, and she will be able to work. Nobody will creep up on her, nobody will call out to her, nobody will want to read aloud to her passages from a book or a newspaper article. She will be alone with her work and only the sounds of shuffling and scraping upstairs, where a woman and her elderly mother live. On a few unexpected occasions the man has stayed out late during the week, and she has hurried into her work at these times, but nervously, because she never knows when the man will arrive home and ask what she is doing. He has a certain way of arriving, throwing the door open as though popping the cork on a bottle, and instantly the house is reorganized because now he is at its center, whereas before she and her work were at the center, and she was traveling through the center of the work, moving slowly, very slowly toward the time when the project will be finished.

One late Sunday morning she is jumpy, thinking about her afternoon and how much progress she might make on her project. She has a feeling that today, if she works diligently, she might come close to finishing. She watches the man preparing for his ride: filling his backpack with food, spare tubes, a bottle of water. He charges his cellphone in case he has an accident and needs to call for help. When they were first living together, she would sometimes daydream that the man would have a terrible accident and not come back for a few days, and in that time she would be able to finish her project. The daydream makes her feel very ashamed now, because the man is kind to her, and he does not like to leave her alone. She no longer allows herself the daydream. But even though she cares for him, and even though she knows he will go eventually and she will be alone this afternoon, she grows more and more anxious for him to leave.

She goes to the spare bedroom and sits at the desk. Over and over she reads a page of her notebook where she has written a list of tasks. The thought of finishing her project floods her with happiness. She can hear the man moving around the house, the sounds of zippers on his backpack, the click of fasteners. He will be leaving in a few minutes. She hears the toilet flushing. She hears him in the kitchen, opening and closing cupboards. Soon she will hear his footsteps in the hallway. He will come into the room to kiss her good-bye, and he might stay for a while to talk to her about the route he plans to ride. On a few Sundays he has begun to talk about other things too, such as his own projects, or what they might have for dinner that night, and on those occasions he has stayed past the time when she would reasonably expect him to leave, and she has felt an increasing desperation to go into her work and has become afraid she might start pulling at her hair, or stabbing at herself with a pen, or tearing at her clothes. Then, just at the moment when her hand is losing strength from squeezing the pen so tightly, he has left her. He has walked up the steps along the side of the house, past the window of her room, to the little door that leads under the house to the dark cramped place where he keeps his bicycle out of the weather.

There was one Sunday, though, just after he walked out the door, when she heard a strange thump and looked up to see him pressed against her window. He was smiling at her from underneath his helmet, waving his arms above his head, and he looked like a giant spider. She knew then: he knew that she wanted to work, and he was teasing her. Then he waved once more, and as always, retrieved his bicycle, then slipped down the road and out to the coast and was gone for some hours.

There is no sound in the house now, even though the man is still there. Her chest has a funny feeling, as though her heart is rippling and growing larger, beginning to blur, dispersing like dye into water. As the feeling in her heart spreads into her arms, it begins to softly fizz, as though she were filled with strange debris. She is ready to go into her work to escape these feelings but she can't hear where the man is. At least twenty minutes have passed since she heard him moving about in the kitchen. The feeling is curling up into her neck and face and eyes, and she feels overcome by it and afraid that she will cry out. Finally she stands.

In the living room, the man is sitting on the couch, in his cycling clothes, even his helmet. He is eating slices of toast. He smiles at her and says he is going soon but that he thought he should eat something first. There are still three slices of toast on his plate and she calculates that it will take him at least fifteen minutes to eat these, for he eats slowly.

She imagines running outside and throwing herself into the muddy ditch at the bottom of the garden, covering herself in cool leaves and grasses, covering herself in another feeling besides the feeling in her heart and her fear that she might stab at herself with a pen or tear her clothes apart. But instead she sits down beside the man and picks up a book that she left lying open the night before. She pretends to read as she listens to the man eating. Each chew is as loud to her as if she were inside his mouth, sliding this way and that, up and down, watching the slick insides of his mouth, and his teeth, which are slightly crowded together, breaking the toast down.

After he has finished the final piece of toast he begins to talk about the ride he has planned. It is always at this moment, when he is telling her about where he will ride, that her impatience and anxiety lift away. It is easy to talk to him when he is about to leave. It is as if they are both standing at a train platform or a gate at an airport—she will go away to her work, he will go away to his ride—and the places ahead of them both, where they will not see each other, feel exciting but also places to be traveled through quickly so that they can return to each other again. In that moment, even though she wants very badly to work now, she looks forward to seeing him again.

The sound of his cleated shoes take a long time to fade as he carries his bicycle over his shoulder up the steps to the road. She waits for a few minutes, making sure. The air takes time to settle in his departure.

Then, she works. She works greedily.

Deep inside her work, she feels her body disappear; she can

travel through the work with grace. She barely notices the sounds of shuffling and scraping overhead as the woman upstairs, perhaps, tries to settle her elderly mother. She works for such a long time that when her body returns, it is in protest; she is tired and hungry. When she looks up, her eyes feel guarded, as if unsure about any sight but work. The clock says that many hours have passed, and indeed the sky through the window is now dim.

For the first time since she began to work this afternoon, she thinks about the man. He was riding all the way around the peninsula, he'd said, and then over a small mountain range. He would ride into a strong headwind and on some parts of the road the waves would come up over the road. He'd told her about the new lights he'd bought that were brighter than all other lights, so bright that they would light up every mark on the road and all the leaves on the trees. She imagines him out there on his own. She decides to take this opportunity to continue to work. As the hours go by, hours and hours, and the man still does not return, and her work goes on before her—slipping always just ahead of her so that she cannot catch it—the feeling in her heart returns, but stronger. Her heart seems to ripple outward like a puddle, spreading so far that it might fill her body completely, leaving her unable to move but for a slow throbbing. Finally she begins to hope that the man might come home soon to relieve her. As she lowers her eyes once again to her work, it is as if her work is looking out at her, pressed up against her hands, refusing to leave her.

can you tolerate this?

When you go to your chiropractor, he first asks you to take off your necklace. Then he stands behind you and puts his hands around your neck. He squeezes the vertebra at the base of your skull. The vertebra feels tender, as if bruised. "Can you tolerate this?" he asks. You try to nod. You hadn't known that vertebrae could reach so far up, right to the back of the brain.

"Oh yes. The vertebrae go all the way up to the head, like a ladder. Humans are really just highly evolved ladders."

You like the idea that the human body is first and foremost a structure, like flat-pack furniture or a foldaway bed. The ribs, too, go up a long way, into the soft fleshy parts of the back near the armpits.

You lie down on the stretcher, which is a low vinyl-covered table with a headrest that has two fabric-covered sausages on each side, into the center of which you put your face. From there, in a muffled voice, you talk to your chiropractor: about the foul spring weather, how you were knocked off your bike last week, maybe how you're thinking of quitting your job.

You've known the chiropractor for two years. He's a nice man. He's someone who, when you say something banal—which is often—reacts as if you've said something extraordinary or very funny. But you're not really paying attention to this conversation. It's the other conversation you're interested in: the one between his hands and your back. Your back feels as if it's listening. You know his hands are close when you feel a tingle in the skin on your back, as if the nerves in your spine are reaching up to the surface.

Your chiropractor begins to knead your spine. You can hear him counting under his breath—T3, T4, T5. Those are some of your thoracic vertebrae, named according to their positions within the spine.

It sounds like torture when you try to describe it to other people. You come here to have your spine shoved or your head wrenched sideways. Better to talk about the lightness and tallness you feel when you leave. Some people are so afraid of chiropractic that they become afraid of *you* if you mention your chiropractor. The difficulty is that a person's life is held, essentially, in the spine. If you mess badly with it, you will die or be paralyzed. Your jaw will seize and your eyes will stare frozenly. For some, chiropractic will never escape those connotations of torture. Mostly it's because we think bones should be silent. When we hear them moving, we think of pain, of permanence.

"Those aren't your bones making that noise," says your chiropractor when you ask. "It's actually gas." It's the sound of tiny bubbles of oxygen, nitrogen, and CO_2—by-products that are formed in the production of the synovial fluid in the joints of the spine. The gas releases from the joint with a *pop*. Nothing ever happens to the bones themselves, the chiropractor says. The bones stay quiet, the introverts of the body.

If you ever ask him a question, it's as if the chiropractor becomes worried that you've grown skeptical and he has to persuade you all over again. So now he explains that the spine is like a scaffold, or a bridge between your nerves and your body, holding all of you upright so that the work of art that is the body can commence motion. He laments the way people say, "I've put my back out," as if a back were something you could hold at arm's length and leave on the curbside. "The problem with people is that they think of themselves as bits and pieces. Go to the gym, work on your pectorals. Work on your quads. A body part here, a body part there. Then we wonder why we feel so disconnected from ourselves. As if your head lives on a different continent from your feet, or your eyes live on a different planet from your heart. Well, for some people perhaps that is figuratively true. But most of us live in the one body, wouldn't you agree? All of those parts are endlessly, infinitesimally connected." He says that if your scaffolding is askew, then the rest of your body and your mind won't work. Things start sliding, shaking, falling. You wake up one morning and you can't move your neck. That's where the manipulations—or, more technically, subluxations—come in. All day long, he is not only fixing but reconnecting.

"I'm not saying there aren't some essential differences between the human body and, say, an airplane. But there aren't very many." He pauses. He's found something, some vertebrae that aren't where they should be. "Deep breath in—and deep breath out—" and he pushes your spine so hard it crackles electrically.

He has you roll to the left. He rearranges your arms so that you're in a relaxed fetal position. Then he presses one of his knees against your thigh—he has large square knees that dwarf your smallish round ones—and pushes. There's a faint cracking sound, like roots pulling up. You imagine fissures appearing in your body as if during a quake.

"Can you tolerate this?"

You keep your eyes half closed but you can see him looming above you like a pylon. "Yup. I'm fine." You roll to the right and he cracks open the other side.

Sometimes, when you're lying here having your vertebrae prodded, he will ask you a question. The question will be big and difficult. It will be something like, "What do you think is the difference between a thought and an emotion?"

You will struggle to answer. But you try to sound as if you think about this kind of thing all the time, as if you're on a slightly different time-space continuum from everybody else. "Well, a thought is only ever in your head. An emotion can be, I don't know, in other places in your body. It can be everywhere.

It's kind of shapeless and fluid. It can feel almost physical, like a pain." Your voice sounds all wrong against the stretcher.

He never agrees or disagrees with what you say; instead he pauses for a moment—you can feel him thinking, through his hands—and then says something like, "Could you say, perhaps, that an emotion is a physical thought?"

Immediately you wish you had thought of this. "Exactly! An emotion can make you feel sick or sweaty or excited, and those are all like physical expressions of different thoughts."

Talking like this makes you wriggle around, and your chiropractor gently straightens you out or puts your arms back down at your sides.

In the past, like most people, you thought that seeing a chiropractor was an absurd risk. It wasn't until a friend at work, telling you about his own pain, persuaded you that there was something good in this method—something that really worked, maybe even something transformative—that, being desperate with shoulder pain, you decided to reconsider.

At first, it felt like a mistake, this blind trusting of a person, much bigger and stronger than you, with your life. But when you're stretched out on this vinyl table, when your chiropractor puts his hands on your back and tells you what he knows about your bones, then the idea of risk becomes only that: an idea. Something rootless. There's something else, too. This feeling that happens when you are touched. It is a kind of trust in itself. Trust is something that moves about between you, that rises to meet him.

"That back is good to go. Sit up now," he says. You do, fuzzy-haired, squinting; your eyes have adjusted so quickly to the facedown darkness that they feel splintered by light from a window. The sun is angling in. The egg-colored elasticated spine is hanging in the corner. "Let's take a look at that neck of yours."

He looks down at you and takes your head in both hands. He presses your throat just under your jawline, the bones at the base of your skull, and the tender spots under your ears. He gazes over the top of your head. You can't help thinking at this point that, maybe, he will lean down and kiss you. That he will frame your face with his hands and engulf your mouth, warmly, and the office space and the spine hanging in the corner and the anatomical posters on the walls will disappear. There is too little difference between the beginning of a kiss and the beginning of a neck adjustment. You stare at his face, waiting, breathing through your mouth.

After a final pause, he yanks your head to the left—*snap*— then to the right. The sound is a sheet of bubble wrap popping. Your chiropractor steps back and nods, finally looking you in the eye. Now that he's out of your personal space, he is safe.

"You're good at those," he remarks with a wry smile. "Most people scream a little bit."

You try out your new neck: it feels freer, oilier, as if all the synovial fluid has been released to flood over the joints in there. And your head sits more lightly, an egg balanced in a spoon.

But wouldn't it be easier to simply feel nothing? It wouldn't be a problem if you could think of your body as an airplane, as your chiropractor does, or simply a lattice of sinew and bone, muscle, soft tissue, nerve fibers. A body with an ordinary skeleton inside it; it could be anyone's, it could be one of those pink-and-white posters on the wall, bristling with pointers and labels.

To mask your lapse, and perhaps to redeem yourself to your chiropractor in case he has sensed what you were thinking during the neck adjustment, you quickly ask another question even though this will hold him up. "Do you ever get annoyed about skeptics? I mean, do you have people who come in and say they think it's all phony but their friend told them to come, that kind of thing?"

"Oh," he says—and you can hear the pragmatism in his voice; he's used to being the reasonable, rational one among the disbelieving—"there's certainly a lot of folklore around. People think they've slipped a disc. They think they've got a nerve floating around in their spine, you know, just drifting around in there. Sometimes when I treat people's backs, they think I've broken them in half! Or they think I'll give them a stroke or a heart attack. But look, I don't waste my energy getting frustrated anymore. You have to look above all that stuff. You have to work above it."

You take your necklace from his desk and put it back on. You always feel a little awkward doing this; this small, intimate putting-on in your chiropractor's office. Briefly you are a woman in a movie.

He is shuffling the pages of his appointment book. "How are you for next Thursday at noon?" Between his eyes is a hearty furrow. How old is he? You're no good at guessing age. The whites of his eyes are properly white, not like the whites of most eyes, which are singed with vessels or nicotine-yellow; in most eyes you can see what people have been looking at: traffic, computer screens, TVs. You find yourself staring at his skin. You can imagine him in one of those multiblade razor ads, the kind where a fighter plane is tearing through the sky. Its body explodes to reveal your chiropractor tensed and helmeted at the controls; the air resistance rips his suit from his body to reveal his bare torso, then he is neatly deposited in an incandescent bathroom as a razor darts through the air and slots into his hand. His face, now magically slathered with shaving foam, appears above the razor.

"Thursday's good for me."

After paying up—twenty-five dollars for fifteen minutes, which you can't really afford—you smile good-bye and he puts his hand lightly on your shoulder, as if placing a full stop there. He is a genuinely nice man. He is interested in people: their bones, their physical thoughts. And you feel the thing you so often feel when you meet someone like this—that you have done nothing to deserve this niceness.

When you're walking down the stairs, you feel a suspicious glow in your belly. It's then you realize: you've got to stop this. Your chiropractor is a mechanic and you are a vehicle in occasional need of repair. When being helped, that is all we need to be. A hairdresser touches hundreds of heads. A doctor listens to hundreds of hearts. None of that means anything beyond what it is.

A month or so down the line, you're greeted at the office by a young woman with a shiny brown ponytail. Your usual chiropractor is away today. The woman has strong hands and enviable self-confidence. She adjusts your lower back, hips, neck, and the sticky-outy rib that is causing your sore shoulder. You leave feeling slightly delirious.

At your next appointment, she tells you that your usual chiropractor is in hospital. He has a tumor. "I just wanted to let you know," she says. "It's early days yet. He's doing fine. We'll just see what happens."

You think of your chiropractor in hospital, waiting for tests, waiting to see what happens. Who does he trust with his life? You wonder what it would be like to visit him. You could take flowers, a book, a card. But, of course, you don't visit. He will already have so many visitors. He will be tired. He will need to sleep between visits.

At each appointment over the next months, the new chiropractor tells you he's doing okay. Then she stops mentioning him, and simultaneously you just stop wondering. It's as if some part of you has decided that he will no longer appear in your life and is shutting down the wondering mechanism. Your new chiropractor has warm, friendly eyes and a ready smile. She knows the parts of your neck that store tension in gnarls (she has something called an activator gun—it looks like a syringe from hell—that she shoots into each side of your neck); she knows all about the wayward rib; she knows that there are two muscles on either side of your lower spine that are always sore. At first you'd thought they were your kidneys. Sometimes it seems that you don't know your body at all. The names and locations of things. You need someone else to tell you what your body is doing.

.   .   .

At the vegetable market the air is cool from a night of rain. Broken stalks and leaves are scattered on the asphalt among the stalls. People gather and bend and fill seamy plastic bags. You're looking for tomatoes when you see your chiropractor, your old one, bending toward a crate full of apples, sorting through them. You hold back for a second—this could be weird and awkward— then say hello. He looks at you for a few seconds, searching, then straightens and smiles and says hello back. "How are you doing? How's that neck?"

"Pretty good. I'm keeping it in line." Then you go shy and fumbling. "I heard that you've been unwell. How are you?"

"I'm fine now," he says, nodding. He does look fine, if you look at the surface of his face and don't know about the tumor, which must be gone now. His eyes look bright and clear. He has grown a goatee. No longer will he be the jet man in the razor ad. You think how good it is to see him. You talk about the abundance of cheap avocados—three for two dollars. There are new stalls at the market and now you can get crêpes and pies and beer. You mention the book he once recommended to you, *A New Earth* by Eckhart Tolle—which you'd thought was partly interesting and mostly silly, but which you say you liked. He's holding a canvas bag with bushels of celery sticking out the top. There is very little movement in his body. He stands quite stiffly with his head bowed toward your mouth. Then there's a quiet moment and the wind picks up as it always does, so you say, "Okay, well." He says it was good to see you and puts his hand on your shoulder. Then you each wander away to different stalls.

You have a minor current of electricity buzzing on your shoulder from where he put his hand. You mindlessly spend the rest of your money on half a pumpkin and two kūmara that are so large they look mutant; huge, dark gnarled things with frizzy antennae, they look like they should never have come up out of the ground. Now you have to eat them, and you've spent all your money. Your chiropractor floats into your head at odd moments during the next few weeks. Small, boring thoughts, like, I wonder what he made with the celery, and What is a tumor made of? But a few months later, when you go to see the new chiropractor to sort out your neck, which has seized up from too many hours sitting at your desk, she tells you, with mist in her kind eyes, that he has died.

absolutely flying

Of all the senses, sight must be the most delightful.
—*Helen Keller*

L ate one night my brother JP woke to a flashlight shining in his face. "Who's that?" he said, sitting up, reaching for his glasses as if they were a gun. But they weren't on his bedside table. His heart began to pound. What if the intruder had a knife? The light slipped away and there was the sound of footsteps thumping down the stairs. JP scrambled out of bed. Without his glasses he was legally blind, and—he realized halfway down the stairs, in the chilly hallway air—naked. He gripped the banister and felt his way with his feet, but he wasn't quick enough. The door slammed, and as JP was stepping to the ground he tripped on a stack of phone books and fell to his knees. He picked himself up, threw open the door, and ran out onto the street, naked, panting. Nothing but foggy streetlights and the glow of houses. "I wanted to say, 'Hey, you can't do that! You can't just come into people's houses.' But I couldn't give chase."

Now that he thinks of it, he tells me, just yesterday he was cycling down Adelaide Road at rush hour, and all of a sudden he was blinded by a piece of flying grit. It is so easy to be incapacitated at a moment when you really need to see clearly in front of you.

As a boy, JP could often be found kneeling on the floor with a flashlight. Up close, the shag carpet was a forest. Soon the five of us were crouched there, moving only when absolutely necessary—and slowly, slowly—our heads huddled around the spot where the contact lens was believed to have fallen, a silent parachute dropped into no-man's-land. "Get her out of here," Dad roared when the dog came trotting in, suddenly huge and hairy before the delicate operation. Finally someone would spot it—*There!*—crumpled on a tuft of carpet. Or dotted on the edge of a chair, or more often, attached to the front of JP's shirt like a hangnail. Lenses were very rarely truly lost. One lens was worth a lot of money. At the Hamilton optometrist, JP would sit in a darkened room and wear metal headgear like RoboCop. The optometrist dropped an alien green dye into his eyes. The dye oozed from his eyes down his cheeks; it looked like he was crying radioactive tears.

My brother Neil's eyes are still good. They are excellent. They are of fighter pilot quality. He has been lucky in that regard, he says.

.   .   .

There is a man I see most days. He has a jaunty walk and a beatific smile inside his beard. He taps his stick deftly on the ground. The stick is something like an elephant's trunk: a sensing, thinking extremity with a nubbin on the end. The man can maneuver his way neatly around obstacles—sudden curbs, fallen road cones, upended shopping carts, recycling bins. Nearby there is a foundation for the blind, so that each morning you see a number of others who are visually impaired, young and old, towed by dogs or white tapping sticks. There is one woman who doesn't wear dark glasses. She taps her way along the path with the same jaunty walk as the man, her long coat swinging, her hair an aureole around her face. Her eyes flutter electrically, trying to stay closed or open.

The term good eyes resonates for me in the way *my own house* or *a full head of hair* must resonate for others. My eyes were good at first. Then they slowly became less good, and within the space of about two years, they became bad, so that sometimes, sitting at the back of a classroom and searching the blackboard, I felt scared, as though not being able to read it meant I couldn't process language anymore.

When my first pair of glasses arrived, I left the optometrist and walked down the street like someone who had awakened in the future. There had been many new developments I might never have known. People's eyelashes, their blemishes, the buttons on their shirts. When people saw me staring they looked away. I'd forgotten the rule about not looking too long. Even the trees had secret leaves, as detailed as fine woodcuts. There was a vigor in the detail. Light didn't come from the sun, after all, but from things and people. It came from roads and roadside gardens, from couriers on bikes zigzagging across the footpath; it came from movement.

As well as staring at people, I liked to take my new glasses off and on. Off, on; blind, sighted; absent, present. It was difficult to settle into the new eyes. But the more I allowed myself clear sight, the less I truly understood what it was that I saw, because the new detail lent a certain strangeness to things I thought I had seen many times before.

I could see the expression on my mother's face as she trudged back from the garden, could see her mouth slightly moving as she spoke to herself. What was it she was saying? I could see clematis struggling with the old man's beard in the bush; I could see new aerials on Ben Lomond. And on my way home I could now clearly see the man down the road who sat low in his car and watched me as I walked past.

New parts of the world had been sifted out and held up, glinting. At night, despite my glasses, the Te Kūiti lights still looked like landed UFOs.

"Hang on. I think I can see it. It's right in the back there."

My father held up JP's eyelid and shone torchlight into the recesses.

It felt dangerous. We could be here forever, JP's head craning back, Dad peering into the eye. The lens was too far gone, as if lost on a roof in a faraway neighborhood.

"I just think we should ring the optometrist, Russell." My mother was hovering in the doorway.

"Hang on, hang on—"

"I'll do it!" JP hit Dad's hands away and bent over the desk, sluicing out his eye with saline solution—sluicing, blinking, rubbing, until finally the lens appeared on the towel on the desk. A beaten-down thing, like a scrap of albumen.

Contact lenses made JP's eyes sensitive to sunlight. To counteract this he had to wear sunglasses. At primary school in the playground, he sat on a bench quietly by himself. It was safer to stay in one place, eyes in the dark, watching all the eye-unfriendly activity whirling around—people pushing one another over on the asphalt, tennis balls thwacking flesh.

He had a special way of putting the lenses in. With his right hand he took a lens from the case. He held it up to the window to get the light. He opened his mouth wide, pulling his upper lip down over his teeth. This silent howl stretched his face to provide easier access to the eye. He held one eye open with the thumb and forefinger of his left hand. He moved the lens toward the wide-open eye, and like magic, with a blink, it was gone. The eye gulped it up like a fish. He closed his mouth and blinked away the saline tears. His face always looked startled as the world rushed in.

"Having bad eyes makes you observant," JP tells me now. "You don't trust your eyes so you're always checking to see what they can see." It was the things he couldn't see that always caused him pain: a mailbox he bumped into, giving him a bloody nose; our cat in the hallway, hunting for legs. "I would have to say that my lenses—and those moments when they pop out or cause sudden bursts of pain—have caused me more trouble than good. Would I rather live with bad eyes or live with lenses? I don't know. I'd rather just have good eyes."

When he was working for Colorado Mountain Express, every day JP drove a van full of tourists down to Denver in the snow. On the way he would see cars and trucks and vans smashed into walls where they had spun off the icy road. Not long before he left the job, another driver slid off the road and into the path of a snowplow. The driver was okay, but his passengers were not. Nine of them ended up in hospital and one woman broke her back.

"One night, at about one in the morning, I was on my way from Denver back to Vail," he says. "I had a vanload of people. It was snowing heavily and the interstate was treacherous and icy. Most people in the van had fallen asleep by that point of the night—they were university students on holiday to the snow.

"I was coming down the last mountain road before reaching Vail Valley, and the road became steep and spooky. It was like driving down into Ngauranga Gorge, but steeper and icier. Suddenly, one of my contact lenses popped out! Just like that— *blip!*—I was blind in one eye."

All of his depth perception was gone. He could no longer see how close he was to the concrete barrier or to the vehicles in front of him or to the vehicles piled up behind. On the snow and ice you cannot put your brakes on whenever you want to. If you do, you might spin out and end up against a wall or in a valley upside down, hanging from your seat belt, passengers around your ears. So he stayed as he was, eyes streaming. His hands froze to the wheel as he ghosted down the valley road. The freight trucks pressed down behind him. Lights lapped over the windshield. He hardly breathed. The van slipped and slid on the ice beneath him, making up its mind whether to let him stay or go. Inside, all was quiet except for the *swoosh, swoosh* of passing vehicles. And then, like a dream, he found himself pulling into the visitor center, too shaken to be glad he was alive.

"I opened the doors in a daze and all the heedless groggy students shambled unsuspectingly off the van and off into the night."

On the other side of the world I must have been going about just as heedlessly, probably working at the shop or eating in front of the TV, or running. I think how strange it is that growing up you feel you are keeping up, step by step, with your brothers or sisters and you feel you'll never really fall behind. But then you fall behind. You have to go backward to things that happened years before. You have to imagine your way there. JP is sitting here in front of me, but he is also behind the wheel of the van coasting silently down a hill.

With glasses, the bad eyes get in at the corners, and the space above your nose when the glasses slide down in the sweat or the rain, and the tops of your cheeks when your drop your gaze. You could almost trace with a finger the seam between your bad eyes and your good. So, after wearing glasses up until I left high school, I decided to get contact lenses.

"Just relax, now," said my optometrist. "If you relax you won't feel a thing."

He pulled back my eyelid and I felt my pupils dilate. As his finger moved toward me, light shone down the back of my head. My eyes jammed shut. They were strong. They could defeat a man's hand. When I opened up, the optometrist was still leaning forward, looking at my eyes as if they were bait.

"It's like putting on an artificial leg," I joked. "Or a respirator." The optometrist didn't smile. But the more I thought about it, the more I thought this was true. Suddenly an artificial device must do this intimate work for you: walking, breathing, seeing. You need to submit. You have to let yourself become feeble without it. I began to explain this to my optometrist but I could sense his impatience, his hands twitching again, so I trailed off into a half chuckle and willed my eyes to be still, just as many years before I had silently begged my dog to keep still on the vet's examination table.

This time the optometrist held my eye open, his fingers pushing back my eyelashes. It felt as though my whole body existed in that one eye and I was just under its surface.

I remembered being in a pool, drifting through foggy water. My head was bumping the sides. I saw a fluorescent ring on the bottom of the pool—the ring I had been trying to reach before I fell—and the grimy seams along the sides of the pool. I was calm. I didn't need to breathe. My lungs and body seemed to have dissolved. All that was left were my head and eyes. The water was a cradle, rocking me. Then I heard a dull crash and the water began to sway. I saw my mother in the water, pale and weedy in her underwear. Her arms reached and closed around me and we rose to the surface. The water streamed away from us. Green trees grew up around the pool, and the wooden house of my aunt and uncle soared upward in the garden.

With lenses in, I could do things at speed. Sprint down hills, ride my bike through the tunnel with lights flying past like Frisbees—I had wind flying around my face, over my eyes, my eyelashes, and I could see. My peripheral vision was like lightning. Nothing could escape. When I looked at a friend, I felt as if not only my eyes but my whole face were opening a door to find her there: her face was frank, her hair was brighter than ever—how had I not understood this before? Part of me had seen it, but now all of me saw it. I stopped bending my head when I walked. It was as if I was climbing. I challenged the world to show me something I couldn't see. I challenged myself to lose something precious so that I could find it again.

Having bad eyes is a fact that wants so badly to be a metaphor for something else. It wants to be the blurriness that prevents people from seeing one another, their inability or refusal to come into focus in one another's eyes. But more often, it is simple, inconvenient fact.

One weekend I stay with my parents, and on the night I arrive, I take out my lenses and leave them in their case next to my father's. When I go into the bathroom the next morning, my lens case is empty. Only the saline pools remain. I dabble my finger into them, just to be sure, but they are gone. Immediately I remove the lids on my father's case. His lenses are still floating there. My father has taken my lenses and, presumably, is now wearing them instead of his own.

"He's out flying," Mum says when I ask where Dad is. "He's back this evening. They're having a picnic in Fiordland." She pauses. "What's happened?"

Have I made a mistake? I go back to the bathroom and try on the other set of lenses, the ones in Dad's case, to make sure they're definitely not mine. But my vision buckles and everything inverts, like water swirling down a sink.

I look around the monstrous room. I take out Dad's lenses and put on my glasses. My vision finally clear, I tell my mother, "There's been a mix-up."

"Good God," Mum is saying, "I thought he looked a bit funny when he set off." But now she seems unconcerned, turning to wipe the bench and nudge some stray cat food back to its bowl with her foot. My parents always assume that the other is safe. Misfortune—serious illness, vandalism, redundancy—happen to other people. These are things to glance at as you pass, and to look away from. So far, this system has worked out well.

My father is an experienced pilot. Even if he really is wearing my contact lenses, even if somehow, in a state of profound absentmindedness, he didn't register the mistake the moment he inserted the lenses, he'll know what to do. With luck he'll be flying with Peter, a middle-aged Rotarian who has lived through two light plane crashes. Or if there is no Peter, maybe his pilot's intuition will kick in like a spare fuel tank and bring him in to land. In the past he has said, *You don't really need to be able to see a whole lot when you're up there: all you need is your GPS*; besides, he has flown over this land for decades and it has not changed very much. I tell myself all of this, but still a tingle creeps over me. I imagine him up there in the blind space, the windshield a smudge of gray, no birds, no hills, no lines of rivers or railway lines, no houses; his own hand a paw.

I try to picture him coming into the house unharmed. He'll have an unfocused look on his face, but this is usual. He will cut a slab of cheese to put on a cracker. As he munches he will describe the blue calmness of the day, the sea like an apron ironed flat, and he'll say the thing he always says after a good flight, and which my mother sometimes repeats: "It was like being on a magic carpet!" He will give me back my lenses, my precious last pair, which he will have stored in a spare case in his pocket. "Like a magic carpet."

In the afternoon I stand in the backyard by the clothesline, looking up, shading my eyes and glasses, as if by some magic I will be able to spot the tail and wings of the Cherokee, a tiny power plug. The sky is empty. It is like something has blown apart and left a hollow. Still I look and look. Especially in the case of the sky, the harder you look the less you see. I keep looking. I don't want to imagine myself backward to what might have happened as I slept, as I stood in the kitchen watching the kettle boil. I'm looking for the plane, for its wings in relief.

sea of trees

An experience of remoteness, space, natural
quiet and solitude is gained standing amongst
the extensive dunes against the vastness of
the Southern Ocean.
—*New Zealand Department of Conservation*

It will be a long tunnel for us.
—*Masahisa Okuyama, father of a hikikomori*

I n the photograph the young man is sitting cross-legged on
a bed, holding a sword across his knees, almost like an offering. In another photograph he holds it loosely across one
shoulder. On a table in the room are a clutter of soft drink bottles, food packets, and cigarettes; in one corner is a pile of bulg-
ing garbage bags. The young man looks directly at the camera,
his eyes clear. He is a hikikomori—a young Japanese person,
usually a man, who has shut himself into a bedroom or flat for six
months or more, sometimes years, sometimes decades. (The

Japanese word *hikikomori* combines the words *hiku*, or "pull," and *komoru*, or "retire"; literally it means "pulling in and retiring.") In other photographs of hikikomori I've seen, the young person turns his back, or is pictured in profile staring into the middle distance. His face is usually obscured and his posture suggests shame. But there is an openness in this young man's face that is at odds with his cloistered surroundings. He could be looking forward to something. He could be about to stand up, swing a pack onto his shoulder, and open the door.

There is another photograph of a hikikomori wearing a hooded sweatshirt with a kind of elongated balaclava, almost like a trunk, that stretches from his face to the computer screen. He doesn't trust his own eyes—they might stray to the bedroom around him, crowding him in—so this clunky portal keeps his focus trained. His body looks like an encumbrance to him, something to be blanked out or wished away. On a hikikomori support website, members are asked how they kill time. The replies advise the Internet, music, sleep: "I sleep until my eyes are about to rot. I see dreams." Immersion is the desired state. It's an escape from physical surroundings, from the passing of time, from worried parents, from the world outside. These replies echo the idea of renouncing or throwing away the self, a state that Buddhist monks are trained to achieve. To be free of the self is to be free from worldly attachments, from uncertainty, from confusion.

The urge to understand or at least to describe makes us liken hikikomori, or "shut-ins," to islands—remote, generating their own weather, enclosed by an inhospitable environment against which they barricade themselves: pulling down blinds, covering windows with black paper and duct tape. If not likened to islands, they are peninsulae, or "almost islands," because many hikikomori do maintain a thread of connection with the world beyond their bedrooms. They live in the homes of their parents, who bring them meals every day, who worry about them, who worry about what others will think, who wonder what they could have done to stop their child from shutting themselves in. Inside their rooms, hikikomori play video games, read, listen to music, drink, pace, or do nothing. Or they surf the Internet, latching on to online communities and forums, networks through which they can connect with others who have withdrawn. In one online support community run through Daizenji Temple near Kōshū City, Yamanashi, hikikomori can meditate with a Buddhist priest who instructs them through an online camera. Some keep their identities hidden by putting on masks, and those who are afraid to be seen at all meditate without using the camera.

The Internet is also a place to pool knowledge about a state that is not often openly discussed. "It's important to make them not frightened," writes a member of the Q&A site Quora in reply to the question *Any advice or ideas on how to deal with a hikikomori?* "If there's something terrifying, make it nothing. And then try to let him know what the outside world is." The person answering this question is himself a hikikomori, he says, or "soon to become one."

Hikikomori seem to vanish from the world, so it is hard to know their true numbers. A 2010 survey for the Japanese Cabinet Office came up with an estimate of nearly 700,000, but some psychiatrists—including Tamaki Saitō, who gave the condition its name in 1998 with the publication of *Hikikomori: Adolescence Without End*—believe that the figure is well over one million. We know that cities can be places of profound loneliness and social disconnection. We know that in dense communities, when commuting, when working, when trying to sleep, people withdraw into themselves to cope. But the reality of so many people hidden away, as if in a forest, gives a sharper, more unnerving edge to that understanding. It threatens our conception of what it is to be a human being living in the world, what it is to be one of the numbers who inform the present and the history of a place. (We can warp what we see, too. One fashion blog portrays hikikomori as if it were a clever kind of solution: "In times of recession, many young Japanese simply stay home. They personalize little rooms at the top of milquetoast suburban houses in exaggeratedly eccentric ways.") Last year I was struck by the photographer Michael Wolf's depictions of people compressed into Tokyo trains at rush hour—beautiful but ghostly images of faces behind streaked glass—which showed the ways in which people tend to endure agitating conditions: by retreating into themselves, eyes squeezed shut, bodies stiffened against walls or windows.

My own experience of self-imposed isolation is brief, but vivid. At high school, deeply shy, I tried to make myself disappear at morning breaks and lunchtimes. For some months I would go to a dressing room behind the stage in the assembly hall, where my art class was stretching, and later painting, some canvases. To get to the room you had to clamber up onto the stage and duck behind the curtains into the left wing, past reams of moth-smelling gym mats and a clutter of music stands, then jam the key into the lock before someone saw you. There was a long narrow window, where I could see people's feet as they walked past outside. I would lie on the wooden bench in the room and watch the feet, or stare at the blank stretching canvases. I was unable to read or write because of a constant low-level anxiety that I would be found, and the anxiety produced a focus that was too acute to translate words into sense—but pictures and sounds stretched and shimmered like blown glass. As the months went on and the canvases grew thick with my classmates' paintings, my mind seemed to drift further and further away from my body in its lumpy green uniform.

Neither the metaphor of an island nor that of a peninsula helps us to imagine the inner world of the isolated. At their heart these metaphors have only their remoteness; they don't provide a path into or out of the state. In their abstraction, they echo, too, an unwillingness to talk openly about the condition of hikikomori. "In polite company, the subject of hikikomori is seldom brought up," the journalist Michael Zielenziger writes in his book *Shutting Out the Sun.* "*Shikata ga nai,* the Japanese say, or 'It can't be helped.'" In Japanese, *mori* is a homonym for "forest," and I find myself going back to the image of a forest as a way of trying to understand what happens when a person shuts themselves in; how their world, so narrowed, might fill and grow so densely that a person becomes lost in it. It is a forest, too, that has become Japan's most well-known site for suicide. Aokigahara forest, also known as the Sea of Trees, lies at the foot of Mount Fuji, four thousand hectares wide. Its trees grow closely together, blocking the wind, and it is home to few animals and birds, so it is quiet. Each year, volunteers who patrol the forest manage to talk people out of taking their own lives there.

When I think of a pathway out of the forest, I think of the path that the Japanese woman Keiko Agatsuma constructed between the cave where she lived and the beach. She built her path out of pieces of driftwood and covered it in washed-up fishnet to stop herself from slipping as she walked down onto the sand. A simple, cursory path made from the materials at her feet.

Agatsuma had arrived in Christchurch with a three-month tourist visa in August 1978. After traveling around the lower South Island, she took a boat to Stewart Island, a heavy backpack on her shoulders. She arrived at Freshwater Landing, where the launchmaster warned her of dangerously changeable conditions and a boggy wetland track to walk across. But she set off alone; I imagine that she didn't look back. The launchmaster later described her as "wiry, tough-looking." It took her two days to reach the Forest Service hut. She began to explore the island, foraging for food as her supply of groceries dwindled, and soon—in Doughboy Bay, just south of Mason Bay—she came across a cave with a high ceiling and overhanging rātā trees that sheltered the entrance from rain. She set down her pack at the back of the cave, where it was dry. She constructed a bed from driftwood and fishing net. She hung colorful buoys in the trees around the entrance.

It's impossible to know for sure why Agatsuma came to such a remote place. Those who spoke to her on Stewart Island—park

rangers, fishermen—said she had mentioned an abusive husband, and a feeling that she did not belong back home; perhaps
that she felt broken apart from others, as hikikomori do. We can
assume that she wanted not only to be by herself, but to feel the
relief of placing a great distance between herself and her home
country, the opposite of homesickness. The cave was a dwelling
only: it offered no particular culture or history, asked no questions of her. However, Agatsuma was to live there for just one
week. Her overstayer status was quickly discovered by authorities, and she was deported back to Japan, traveling with her
brother, who had come to Christchurch to take her back. The
story of her isolation rippled outward. International media were
fascinated by the tale of the "Japanese woman cave dweller," and
she fell into Southland urban myth. She later inspired a short
story, a film based on that short story, and a Noh play—and perhaps all of these works are testament to the symbolic power of
that image of a woman far from home, living inside a cave, as
if in exile. It seems so far removed from the young man with
his blinds pulled down in a bedroom in suburban Japan, but this
is a story, too, that ripples outward, that remains unsolved.

In her essay "Last Call," Larissa MacFarquhar gives a brief
account of a hikikomori leaving a room from which he had not
ventured for many years. To receive help from a Buddhist priest
named Ittetsu Nemoto, the young man has to leave his room and
walk to a remote temple, where he will be expected to articulate
his feelings to this stranger. Nemoto's theory is that people have
to want his counsel enough to make the journey to see him,
otherwise he probably won't be able to help them. The man has
been living as a hikikomori for a long time, and now he has to

leave not only his room but also his city, and walk for five hours. It is the promise of Nemoto's help at the end of this unimaginable journey that pushes him on. As he walks out of his room, through the city, and finally out of the city and toward the temple, he thinks about what he might say to the priest. The account of his journey ends when he reaches the temple—because after all that time walking, and thinking, he feels that he has reached some kind of understanding. What that understanding is, it's impossible to say. But the man feels sure enough of himself that he is able to turn around, without even speaking to Nemoto, and walk back the way he came.

How can a person in isolation make their way back? The paths the isolated must build are yet so modest, using whatever tools they can find—some left by others, some scattered, almost forgotten, within the walls—to help them walk, howsoever briefly, into the world outside.

bikram's knee

I'm here, but nothing.
—*Yayoi Kusama*

All around us women are getting dressed. They are talking to one another while half clothed, laughing and gesturing and moving about. The air in here is heavy with steam and deodorant. The concrete floor is busy with underwear and the contents of sports bags. I'm sitting on the slatted wooden bench wrapped in a towel. I think I'm going to faint soon.

My friend has perfected her method of concealment while

getting dressed. She hunches down and tents her towel around her body, creating a little pagoda. This method is good but it isn't fail-safe: when she dips down to dry off her legs and feet, I glimpse her back, its bones sticking out like knobbles on a conch shell. My faintness is beginning to pass so I have to confront my own need to get changed. I have to get out of my sweaty clothes without baring too much of myself. I face the wall and tent my towel, scrabbling about underneath it like a hermit crab. At some point one half of my towel falls away, exposing me to the room full of women, and something like electricity runs up and down my spine.

On the studio website there is a photograph of the guru folded up with his knees over his head. He looks like a pair of reins. *Sweat, strain, laugh, and do more for your health, body, and general well-being than you ever imagined possible. These 26 postures and two breathing exercises systematically move fresh oxygenated blood to 100% of your body, to each organ, fiber, restoring all systems to healthy working order, just as nature intended.* In this description it seems to me that our bodies are a collection of strange funnels, blood collecting and draining and collecting.

The yoga class, my first, had seemed comically long. The room was heated to more than 100 degrees, and the sweat on each body was prolific. It draped us in beads and rings and links, a kind of chain mail, and it hung on places I wouldn't normally associate with sweat, like shins and the backs of hands. As the heat rose, it was almost as if our bodies were melting, were entering another state, a fourth state of matter. And indeed the teacher's instructions suggested that the postures, or asanas, had transformative power. "In the future, your knees will come back together." "Eventually, as your skeletal structure improves, your whole spine will lie flat on the floor." "Soon you will feel your spine opening up, lengthening, creating space between the vertebrae. Class by class, month by month, year by year."

I hadn't done any of these postures before. I didn't know that the word *asana* designates a posture in hatha yoga, which today is yoga in its very broadest sense but which translates literally as "the yoga of violence or force," and that this "violence" rises from the forceful fusing of opposites. At first, an asana may feel so uncomfortable as to be unbearable. But with practice it becomes easier for the body to bear, until eventually the yogi can hold that asana seemingly without physical effort, even as internally they ache with exertion. The asana allows the attention to come to rest solely on consciousness in that very moment.

The story, or one version of a largely unverifiable story, is that at age seventeen the yogi Bikram Choudhury was lifting weights when he lost his grip and dropped a weight on his knee, shattering the bone. It was a terrible accident; his doctors told him he would never walk again. He refused to accept this and asked to be carried to his yoga teacher Bishnu Charan Ghosh's school in Calcutta.

Ghosh, to whom Bikram had been apprenticed at just five years old, believed that the human body is the temple of a living god. He was famous for his temper tantrums, for his punishment of students—including of Bikram, whom he'd burned with incense whenever the young boy lost focus—and for his "amazing yoga feats." He liked to demonstrate his strength by doing things like twisting a heavy iron bar into a coil, having a man jump onto his stomach from a height of twelve feet, lying down and having an elephant stand on top of him, and having someone drive a car across his chest. When Bikram was a teenager and the youngest-ever contestant to win the Indian National Yogasana Competition, he and his teacher went on tours together, a kind of traveling yoga circus. And now, Bikram believed that Ghosh had the power to help him to heal his knee.

It was true. After six months of an intense exercise regime, the knee was healed and Bikram could walk again. Indeed, he was stronger than before.

The way our yoga teacher told the story of Bikram seemed to suggest that Bikram's knee could represent any broken part of a body. If you refused to accept the final pronouncement, if you were determined to find a way back to strength, nothing was unfixable. And in fact Bikram, propelled by the triumph of his recovery and by a promise he'd made to his teacher that he would take this yoga to the West, left Calcutta in the early 1970s and created an empire of healing through his specially branded yoga schools around the world. What was at first tragic became inspirational. His yoga swept people up, healed them, transformed them.

During the class, the instructor told us that we all hold our fear in our knees. At the root of our inflexibility was a refusal to let go and be free. This process was supposed to hurt.

. . .

My friend has left the changing room and I am sitting, dressed now but sweating into my clothes, on the slatted wooden bench. My blood seems to move slowly, as if glugged through thin straws. I think about all of the slatted wooden benches I have sat upon. Before school swimming sports, staring down at my stomach. Before phys ed classes, motionless with dread. And later, when I began to exercise compulsively, mornings or evenings in gym changing rooms, seated there with elbows on knees, forehead in palms, waiting for the feeling of transformation.

I get up very early to run most days. It can be creepy running in the dark, especially on a certain stretch around the bay on the southern coast where there are no streetlights. You can hardly be sure of the ground beneath your feet. I take high, lunging steps. I run this early because my mind isn't awake enough to protest. It lies dormant as if underground. I also run at this time because I am largely unseen then.

Once, I have a near-collision with another runner, a man about the same size as me, wearing a white T-shirt. We both yell. I can't make out his face, only that he puts his hands up to it. Then we've passed each other and I hear him yell *Sorry* as he runs on into the darkness. I shout *Sorry* back and hear him laugh. For six more kilometers my skin buzzes with the sensation of nearly colliding with someone, the sudden circumvention like a hypnic jerk.

My focus moves outward when I'm running. I'm alert for whatever's coming toward me, what I'm running into, how the path feels under my shoes, how the air feels on my skin. My awareness of myself is quieter then, lulled into something smoother that doesn't catch or jag. It is inside my stomach and heart and lungs, where a pool of energy seems also to lie, lapping and receding.

Yoga is different. It demands a person's undivided presence. It requires that you direct yourself inward, while being outwardly still. The word *yoga* comes from the Sanskrit word *yuj*— to yoke or bind. A person doing yoga is aiming for union with the divine, is aiming to bring together their mind and body and spirit.

I've come to yoga without any knowledge of its philosophy. I have only a desire to free myself from an awkwardness that I experience as something continually toppling and rebuilding itself deep inside me, and from the stark loathing of my body I've felt as long as I could remember; it encases me as seamlessly as my skin. More difficult still to admit is that I hope yoga will change my body in a way that other forms of exercise hadn't, so that I can be satisfied at least in that way.

My friend is a long body in a back corner of the hot room. Everyone in the room lies down this way, on their backs with their heads pointing toward the mirrors. I spread out my mat and towel and lie down. Each time I come here now, I remind myself at the start that the class isn't forever. It's just ninety minutes. Better ninety minutes of suffering than ninety years, the teacher says, parroting a quote by Bikram himself, as if the alternative to this hot room were a lifetime of suffering. But I take the point. Doing yoga for a few weeks now, I'm starting to feel better, looser. Even my breath feels easier.

When the lights come on, we get to our feet, and before the expanse of mirror the class makeup is revealed: our thighs, midriffs, upper arms, hairstyles. We each stand in the middle of our mat and look into the mirror.

Before taking these classes, I could not remember the last time I'd looked into a full-length mirror so steadily. I tolerated small mirrors on bathroom cabinets. I braced myself when a mirror took me by surprise—when my full-length self streamed past on the windows of a bus, or when my face appeared in the mirrors above the shelves of a fruit and veg store, an impostor fruit. But in this room we are commanded to look into our own eyes. We are told, The mirror is your best teacher. The mirror reconnects your mind with your body. It requires you to inhabit your own practice and prevents you from invading the practice of someone else. Without the mirror you cannot balance, in any sense. But it's difficult, looking at it. I'm soft in the wrong places, hard in the wrong places; my face looks like the middle of nowhere.

Our teacher is slim, beautiful, and Californian. By now I'm used to her clipped, unsmiling delivery of the dialogue. She tells us: If you feel faint, sit down and stay still. But do not leave the room. Your goal is to stay in the room for the full ninety minutes. From the front of the room she sweeps her eyes over us all, and begins issuing a stream of instructions. The class moves as one.

Sometimes our teacher walks slowly among us, examining our work, like an art teacher examining easels. Toes and heels together. Lock your legs. Look into your own eyes. Don't blink your eyes. Repetition gives the more surreal instructions a particular gravity. Come up onto your toes like a ballerina. Imagine I am pulling your hair up to the ceiling. Touch your knees with your face. You are a Japanese ham sandwich. From the side, it looks like you are holding a box. Press your legs together. You have one giant leg. Grip your elbows through the sweat. Use your sweat to build your strength. Breathe. *Savasana*. Dead-body pose.

I follow the experienced yogis and yoginis in the front row, but I'm at the point in my practice where I'm beginning to know which asana comes next. The patter comes from the same script that all teachers must memorize, and because the sequence of postures is always the same, it is as though the postures move through us, rather than our bodies moving through the postures. I've learned that the body is merely a stage upon which each asana acts itself out. It is like energy moving through water, forming waves. Or like being run through by a ghost train.

Although the heat has become less oppressive to me through practice, it's still exhausting in a way that makes my body tingle. The science behind the heat seems hazy and is almost certainly understudied. Learning to bear it seems a kind of yogic exercise in itself—*Bikram says: It is not hot,* you *are hot*—and there are some first-timers who pick up their mats part of the way through and leave, usually trailed by an instructor concerned that the newcomer will faint and hit their head on the concrete floor. I hear that the heat makes the muscles more "elastic" to allow for deeper stretching, or that it thins the blood, or that it dilates the capillaries in order to allow more oxygen to feed the muscles, or that it simply makes the heart work harder. And over time, the body is said to acclimatize: it becomes more efficient in the heat, needing less fuel to accomplish the same effort. There are many possible reasons for why, after a class, you feel so good, flushed clean.

At the end of the standing series, we lie on the floor. Sweat is beading on the walls. A little fan burrs uselessly above us. Our bodies shine and drip. When our brief rest is over and the instructor begins to speak again, we all bring our knees to our chests.

In between classes, I disappear to the appointments my GP has told me to keep. I don't tell anybody about these appointments because, apart from it being embarrassing, it would necessitate telling them what the problem is, and I don't know what it truly is, or where exactly it's located. From one appointment grows a branching network of other appointments, each one with another specialist who is well versed in the tricks that young women in particular tend to play on themselves. These trips always hold promise, and sometimes a wave of euphoria rises up in me, overtaking the guilt and loathing of spending this much time and money trying to fix something that at its heart is simple, as simple as rest, as simple as raising a hand to a mouth. Before I reach the office or clinic or examination room, in my head I have it all articulated. The problem stands tall and upright. But I'm not as prepared as I imagine. With the very first question, all the screws fall out and the skeleton comes rattling down.

What have you eaten today?

I need to be asked this question because, like so many others, I've unlearned the basics. I'm prescribed antidepressants as a short-term crutch, and they make me feel calmer but empty, as if I were sitting always on a slatted wooden bench.

How much tofu? The woman is holding up a fist. This much? My heart sinks as if it, too, is made of tofu.

I travel up the Wellington coast on the train to see a counselor at an eating disorders clinic. She dresses only in black and white, and her skin is visible only on her face and hands. She wears high-collared vests, tight sleeves, heavy skirts with frills, thick stockings, black shoes. I deduce that her clothing is a necessary self-defense for her job, her armor against the eyes of the women, mostly young, whom she treats each day. She needs to prize some wisdom out of them, and they won't let it go if they're too conscious of *her* body—because that will make them too conscious of their own bodies.

A part of you knows, she tells me, that it's irrational to cry when you are at a friend's for dinner and your only option is macaroni and cheese. The part of you that knows this is your *wise* mind. You can learn to pay attention to it. Listen when it says, *This is not a big deal.*

At the same clinic, I see a psychiatrist who looks at me with something like cold rage, as if she can't believe I'm continuing to deny my part in an obvious crime. I try to charm her, but she has no patience for it, not understanding that I have nothing else. We share long silences in which I stare at the box of tissues on the table between; over time the shape of the tissue box becomes preserved in my head, like dried flowers.

At the beginning of each session, she has me stand on a set of scales. I look down at the tiny world flickering there. As the number comes to rest, I try to hold it at a certain place with my eyes; if only I can concentrate hard enough I can still it. The psychiatrist leads me off the scale. No change, she announces. You are still restricting. I have given you very specific instructions here, and you are still restricting.

I imagine her throwing my file at the wall—her notes erupting, lists of foods whirling and eddying. I imagine her getting violent, kneeing me in the stomach and getting me in a headlock. I imagine her talking about me with her husband over dinner, their plates full of good, abstract foods. I am so *sick* of dealing with these girls who will not *eat*. Their heads are full of *air*! I imagine him patting her shoulder wearily. But none of that is fair. To really help us, to get us to take it seriously, I know she has to scare us. And sometimes, sometimes, there is a glimmer of a smile. At the end of an appointment, her eyes soften and she looks at me wryly, as if she knows what I am up to and is willing to play along with me for a few seconds. In those few seconds we are friends.

I go to see a naturopath to ask about how I can get more energy. She gives me a bottle with dark liquid in it, with instructions to take it once a day. The naturopath speaks softly and makes no sudden movements. She's like someone who is good with horses. The concern in her eyes has an undercurrent, almost, of panic. One week after my consultation with her, a letter arrives in the mail. She has typed two pages of instructions with sentences such as *I cannot emphasize enough the vital need for pro-*

tein foods to produce the brain neurotransmitters that help to elevate mood and regulate sleep patterns etc. and Siberian ginseng: this is a well-known herb used in Chinese medicine to aid in building stamina and endurance for your body and finally Remember it will take time to make new habits but take one day at a time.

The letter feels precious to me. It's like a letter of advice from a parent to her child in the future. I read it through twice, three times, then tuck it into a desk drawer. I read it again in the following days. But each time, the letter seems less precious, the instructions less applicable to me, and I stop reading them. The letter seems now to be written for someone who is willing and who truly believes what it is she has learned from people who are trying to help her.

Early one morning I undress, put on a green smock, and climb up onto an examination table. Above me is a gray machine like an oversized photocopier. This is the bone density scanner. The radiologist leaves me on the table and goes into a little windowed room. She has me lie still and hold my breath while she takes the scans. There is a whirring noise like a soft current sweeping over. The radiologist asks what I do, and I tell her I'm a student.

Of all the appointments, this is the one I like: the warm whirring room, the soft gown, lying on my back under the machine. I like the light in that room, which is dun-colored and womblike.

This posture digs deep into your body, says the teacher as we lie gasping on the floor after a long second set of the most intense posture of all, camel. If you feel sick, dizzy, or light-headed, it means the camel has found something deep inside your body. It's found something you don't need and gotten rid of it. Farewell! So when you feel sick, celebrate.

This dialogue rolls over me now. I am doing six or seven classes a week. My friend no longer accompanies me. I sweat and lunge around the hot room: head-to-knee separate leg standing, half tortoise pose, camel pose, spinal twist, breath of fire. We ground ourselves into the floor and breathe deeply, fanning our elbows out and up like wings, letting our heads fall back as we exhale. The deep breathing looks like a roomful of people trying to calm themselves down, as if we have received some momentous news and are trying to keep ourselves from losing our heads. I learn to turn myself into a human bow and arrow by balancing on one leg and kicking the other behind me, charging my body forward until I am parallel to the floor, with one arm pointing forward and the other pulled backward by my kicking leg. I learn to fall forward. I learn that even when my vision grows fuzzy black mold at the edges, I can stay upright, that the black mold slowly breaks apart and floats away.

Yoga is exhausting, and sometimes it brings me to my knees, but there is something in it that entrances me, that drenches me in an ecstasy of well-being. I read that, while any vigorous exercise floods the brain with oxytocin, it is yoga in particular that has this effect. And that, indeed, this flooding of oxytocin might play a major role in a person's transformation, as the powerful feelings to which oxytocin gives rise begin to wipe out old neurological links—such as addictions and other compulsive behaviors—that have crippled us in the past.

At the end of class, everybody lies on the floor and the teacher switches off the lights so that we are in the dark. This is *savasana*: dead-body pose. We stay here for a few minutes, tricking our bodies into being dead so that they can absorb all of our work in peace. With your breath, you have to make your heart a snail, as quiet and slow as possible. Each time you come here, murmurs the teacher, you create something new for yourself, create something new for your body.

Sweat sliding into my closed eyes, I picture what this new thing could be. It is like a large, warm, wet stone, with threadlike veins running all through it. It has hinges that enable it to break wide open, revealing a portal where dark jagged things are pulled through as if into a black hole, and somewhere on the other side they are transformed into pieces of light. What is it and where in me is this thing? The teacher talks of the importance of creating space—space between each of our joints, space in our minds, and of course space in each day to practice. By *space* they mean openness and calm. But I can't imagine anything other than a deep, glittering space to be fallen through.

When the teacher leaves the room I always stand up quickly, before anyone else. I tiptoe between the damp heads and spread-eagled limbs and past the darkened mirrors. For a second I look at my reflection. I always look at it for signs of transformation. I glisten and drip as if I've been churned through water. When I see myself standing in isolation, I see then that I haven't created anything new. In the postures, it had felt almost as if I were someone else; that I had withdrawn and somebody else had moved through me. But whatever had felt new only stretches taut and snaps, in the briefest moment of looking.

. . .

What does this tell you, says the psychiatrist. She is tapping the paper in front of her. My GP has sent the results from my bone density scan to her. The results say that my bones are losing tissue and becoming brittle in my back and hips.

Isn't it reversible? I say.

Do you want to have children? Or do you want to be an old woman who needs a cane, who needs a new hip, who walks around all hunched over and curled up?

I see myself as a leaf, curled and brittle. *Porosis* comes from the Greek *poros*, meaning passage, pore. Wrapping my arms tightly over my stomach and chest, I tell her I don't know.

The psychiatrist folds her arms too, to show that my answer is not the right answer. Tell you what, she says loudly, it's not looking good. You better start listening and making some big changes. She raps on the paper so loudly that I flinch and my scalp prickles and I feel stubbornness move in me, rising almost mechanically, like steel.

One of the best yoga teachers at the studio is a young Indian man from London. He's new to this studio but has been teaching for six years. There is a rumor that yoga cured him of leukemia. In classes his dialogue is smooth and unbroken, and he walks fluidly among us. He has a demeanor of total serenity.

One day I ask him about Bikram's broken knee—whether it is true that he dropped a heavy weight on it and was told he would never walk again, but cured himself with yoga before going to America.

Oh yes, the teacher says. The details are of course hard to verify but the story is ultimately true as far as I know. When I did my training, I heard Bikram himself tell the story a number of times.

What's he like, Bikram?

The teacher pauses thoughtfully. He says, Bikram has a reputation for being prickly. But he's a shining example of what you can achieve if you set your mind to it. For a man in his late fifties he's full of youthful energy.

He smiles and looks over my shoulder; fresh students are milling through the door for the next class.

At home in my flat, for the first time, I google the guru Bikram Choudhury. There are many photographs of him teaching his classes. When he teaches he wears a black Speedo and a headset like a pop star, and his hair is in a little topknot. There are many articles about him. He lives in a mansion in Beverly Hills. He has many millions of followers around the world, and each year some of these followers, who have fallen in love with yoga just as I have, decide that they want to teach others. They pay thousands of dollars to go to the outskirts of San Diego to train under Bikram himself for nine weeks and become certified instructors. Bikram presides over them on a throne—a giant, inflatable leather throne—inside a viciously hot tent, beneath his personal stream of cool air. The rest of the tent is so hot that some students break down sobbing, or they pass out, or vomit.

Bikram is described alternately as charismatic, tragic, kind, lonely, cartoonish, megalomaniacal, and cruel. He makes offensive comments about the bodies of women in his classes, ridiculing the overweight and the imperfectly proportioned. He speaks of his sexual conquests. He parades and flexes his muscles. He has the women who work for him massage his feet and brush his hair. He says things like *I have balls like atom bombs, two of them, one hundred megatons each. Nobody fucks with me.*

But his class is described as a laboratory for transformation. An injured man is brought into Bikram's class on a stretcher and propped against a wall; months later, beginning with the smallest movements he can muster, he can do all of the asanas. He is returned to himself.

In class the teachers often preface their aphorisms with *Bikram says*, which usually means we are about to hear something slightly mysterious, utterly abstract, possibly true. *Bikram says this work is not easy, but it is the most rewarding work you will ever do, the only work that will really free your mind and heal your body and soul.* And, *Bikram says that every day your practice is new, because every day you wake up in a different body. You can never reach the end of this yoga practice—it goes on and on and on, for infinity.*

There is a lanky, tattooed instructor who recovered from cocaine and heroin addiction with the help of this yoga and then, after completing Bikram's training, began teaching in studios around the world, before he came to this one. During class, he sometimes fixes me with his ultramarine eyes when I am slacking. What are you doing? I said *pull!* Lock your knees and focus forward! Until you get your forehead to your toes I'm gonna be the pain in your ass. And after that I'll *still* be the pain in your ass.

But when we are lying exhausted in *savasana*, he speaks to us softly about the nature of the self, how it is essential and absolute. How it is the one thing that accompanies us through the transformation of the body, how indeed the self grows stronger day by day, as we do this yoga.

An idea I hear often in class is that within each asana, we must seek stillness. Even as inwardly we are crying, both stretched and contracted, there will be a moment when all effort disappears and we find true stillness. That is the moment, the legendary Indian sage Vyasa said, "when the mind is transformed into infinity." Our stillness, our rigidity, transcends the human condition because it is a refusal to bow to our desire to break out of the posture, a refusal to fall back into the torrent of other states of consciousness. It is a moment of utter suspension.

"He who practices asana must employ an effort that consists in suppressing the natural efforts of the body," writes the philosopher Vacaspatimisra. "Holding an asana embodies the chaos of existence framed within the stability of the universal," writes the competitive yogi Benjamin Lorr.

Once, my tattooed instructor is a student in our class. He is practicing on the mat directly in front of me. The room feels hotter than usual, and in the first posture—half-moon with hands-to-feet pose, *ardha chandrasana* with *pada hastasana*—he is brought to his knees. He slowly bends forward and touches the floor with his forehead. He covers his head with his hands and lies still. He lies there for twenty minutes on his stomach while the class continues on around him. I feel an urge to go over to him, help him up, and take him out of the room. But then he clambers slowly to his feet, and continues.

The counselor says: You have very rigid expectations that have built up over many years. But those expectations are not you. They don't exist, in fact. They are imaginary and quite separate from your real self.

You need to know your warning signs. What do they look like? What do they feel like? How can you help yourself when you see those signs?

Every couple of hours or so, take thirty seconds to ask yourself, *What's going on? How am I doing? What do I need right now?*

What would happen if you didn't do yoga today, if you didn't run today, if you didn't swim, if you ate normally? What would happen if you got up and looked out the window and were still and not afraid? What if you ate a pie?

I look at my dirty nails. I say: I don't know. I say: I would be someone else. Or maybe it would depend what kind of pie.

We go into my childhood. At this point I stop fighting my fear of cliché. I am sitting in a counselor's office telling her about my childhood. Maybe, as while holding an asana, once I learn to refuse my thoughts of cliché, the cliché itself will disappear and I will become real.

I remember hunkering down in my parents' bed as sounds inside the house took on physical volume and became huge, dark shapes that threatened to engulf me. The sound of somebody typing at the computer was gunshot, and the sound of my mother's hands untwisting me from the sheets was trees in a thunderstorm. I remember the sound of my father going swimming very late at night. I remember the bearded man who would watch from the front seat of his car, slouched down low, as I climbed the hill home. I remember the laughter of the boy over the back fence, the laughter of his friends. I know I am distorting these things in the very act of remembering, retelling, writing.

The therapist is wearing a black long-sleeved dress with white lace at the cuffs and hem. She looks like a character from a fairy tale. She tells me she is pregnant and so the following year we will have to stop our sessions, but I can follow up with someone else if I like, and in fact it is in my best interests to do so, as there's still important ground to cover. Not only can I follow up with someone, but I can also come for meals if I want, and I can even consider staying here for a time. She says, You have the option.

I imagine making up a bed here, putting pictures on the walls of a small room, and sharing communal meals with others. Would it be easier to live life apart from life, even for just a small time? I think of Yayoi Kusama, whose art I love. She admitted herself to a psychiatric hospital in 1977 and never left. She created a large sculpture for the hospital yard—a rowboat and oars covered with stuffed canvas protuberances. In the mornings she dresses in her polka dots and walks to her studio down the road.

I have a weird relationship with it, my friend says. It's disintegrated over the years, I suppose, especially over the past few months. It's just stress. I'm glad you understand.

She's talking about her relationship with her body. She covers her mouth as she talks. She looks down at her sandwich. She rubs at her hands, which look raw as if she has been scrubbing dishes with sandpaperingly hot water. She says that more than anything she wants to have children but probably won't be able to.

Girls in school, university, workplaces, flats: we swap stories. None of us ever knows how to respond to another's story, or whether it's appropriate to give practical advice, so we mostly talk about ourselves in return. By doing this we hope that our friend will see that we understand, and are the same. Often this works, sometimes it doesn't; sometimes talking about it leaves me hollow. Talking can never quite touch the strange anxiety of the body; it is gripped too tightly, folded up a hundred times to ensure that it won't open and rise until—if we are lucky—many years later, when finally we are old enough to appreciate our body for the things it is able to do, how it can still grasp and lift, reach the top of a flight of steps, bend to retrieve something dropped.

I tell my friend that the first time I fell in love I felt so ecstatic that I stopped eating. But I could still run. I felt that I had tapped into a new energy source: it was somewhere under my feet in the ground, and it could sustain me. I ran so much that the soles on my running shoes got smooth. I felt I was shedding my old self. Once, after running, I returned to the hostel where I was living to find students gathered silently around the TV. I stood behind them, sweating. On the screen I saw people falling from buildings, ties flapping, bodies tumbling over and over. Then the buildings themselves raced toward the earth, smoke and fire coming after them. The images played over and over, as if even the camera could not believe what it was seeing. Neither could I believe it. I could feel the horror of it prickling me, as if it were about to break through and rush over me, but it still couldn't crack the shiny surface of my mania.

All through the next days and weeks I felt a frantic humming under my skin that compelled me to run. Hunger, when it finally surfaced, manifested as a deep ache. The humming was no longer as easy to detect. I tried to spark it again by thinking about the first time I'd held my boyfriend's hand. People seemed to speak to me from very far away. I read the newspaper, trying to take in what was happening. I slept little. When my boyfriend split up with me, the surface finally broke. The world rushed in. I found my old self waiting for me.

My friend puts her hand on my shoulder. We walk out into the square, where some teenagers are break-dancing to a stereo. One of them spins around on the top of his head for whole seconds.

My fixation with yoga perplexes my new boyfriend. As I disentangle myself from the bed and search for my yoga clothes, he says, You can't go to the class today. I've locked all the doors.

I'll climb out the window, I say.

The yoga place is closed.

It is not.

Yes. I rang. I asked.

You're lying.

They said you've been banned for farting in class. You can't go anymore.

I grab his feet and try to pull him out of bed. I say, You have to come with me. You have fear in your knees.

He emits a long groan and rolls over, tugging himself free. Never, he says. I will never, ever, ever come to yoga. He stretches across the bed in a blissful starfish as I put on my shoes.

He is built like a pipe cleaner. His arms are longer than mine. He walks as if he has springs in his legs, like the private eye of the eighties cartoon show *Inspector Gadget*. He only ever wears jeans, emphasizing his thin legs. At first it's hard to imagine his legs naked, like his jeans are his skin and muscle, and I'm unsettled when I see his legs: they are ordinary legs. He takes pride in his ability to make his sternum click, which he does by rolling his shoulders back and breathing deeply. A few gray hairs glint at his temples. He drinks Guinness from a can. He eats fast and often. He plays Ultimate Frisbee. He likes to examine a purple scar on his hip bone, his relic from a skateboarding accident one year ago. Occasionally pieces of grit come out of the scar, delighting him. It is as if his body exists purely to entertain him.

The wall above his desk in his room is plastered with printouts of letters from the typeface he is designing; they spell out *hamburger*. His typeface is named Weka, because the small, hungry running bird epitomizes what he wants his typeface to be, something quick-moving and pointy. He sees each shape in terms of how well equipped it is to convey a message. He spends all his scrutiny on letters, colors, and layout, not people, and so he asks no difficult questions of me, and I am grateful to be left alone at the same time as being held. When we stretch out alongside each other, I imagine my skeleton and his skeleton. His strong, tall, and white; mine a little shorter and narrower, with microscopic passages in the bones: porous. I cling to him.

There is a story that Bikram's wife, Rajashree, sleeps in *supta vajrasana*: fixed firm pose. She kneels on the bed, hips on her heels. She puts her hands on the soles of her feet and lowers herself backward, one elbow after the other. Her head touches the mattress, then her shoulders, and then her whole upper body slides down onto the mattress. She takes hold of her elbows over the top of her head and arches her back, creating a perfect human bridge. She goes to sleep, and every morning wakes up brand-new.

I think about that story as I cycle to my class. How would you hold your body in that asana all night? How would you trick your body into feeling that this was normal? *Supta vajrasana* isn't a difficult posture if your knees have regained their full range of motion, but it's not a comfortable posture; none of the postures truly are, perhaps not even *savasana*, in which you must lie utterly still and ignore any urge to scratch or wriggle about. I'm not sure I believe the story. I'm not sure anyone's body would allow this, especially if her husband was sleeping relaxed and unfurled beside her.

At first, stopping my medication is like the rush of forgetting that happens immediately after an exam. It leaves you like a single breath. As days pass I begin to feel short, hot sparks inside my head. I go to yoga again and again, hoping to dampen the sparks. I know that the tattooed instructor went through drug withdrawal in the hot room; surely I can do the same when withdrawing from SSRIs. My theory is that with yoga I am stronger than I have ever been; I no longer need any medication. I no longer need anything but yoga. With each spark there is a feeling that I'm falling backward through my head—there is so much space to fall through—and jolting onto a different floor of my body. I think about how it was when I first began yoga, how I learned to be unafraid of falling, and how I learned that I could stay upright even when my vision darkened. It's the same process now, only this is a slightly different falling and a slightly different darkening. And the yoga is still working. After a class, I feel more upright. The sparks are leaping, but I have to be patient. I have to look steadily into the mirror, and keep my mind still as my body moves in front of me.

My mother is stroking my arm as I lie in the open doorway to the porch. My legs are stretched out on the paving stones and my feet are in the grass. Our blind cat, Wilbur, is lying against my left ankle. It's Christmas and I'm home, and already I'm thinking of the day after tomorrow, when I can leave and go back to yoga. I feel slightly weaker already, without it. And there's something else, too—a sense of my body starting to become unruly, starting to exist on its own terms, without my routines to keep it in line.

My mother is exclaiming about the hair on my arms. Look at this arm! So hairy.

I remind her that my arms have always been hairy. I remind her of the old photographs of me holding the dog, and how what you notice isn't the dog, but my weird hairy arms around the dog.

She says, Yes, I suppose they have. They're so soft.

I haven't sprawled like this for a long time, outstretched on the ground like the Selfish Giant. In the watercolor picture book, the Selfish Giant lies among white blossoms and a small boy weeps beside him. My father once read me this story before bed, replacing the word *blossoms* with the word *bosoms* throughout, so that the story seemed funny to him but lost all meaning. As I lie here realizing how bizarre this was, my mother begins to talk about her garden. She has been working hard to prepare for a touring day when gardeners from around the area will arrive en masse. She segues into an account of visiting some old friends, buying a kayak from a junkyard, and the possibility of starting up a bed-and-breakfast for vineyard workers and cherry pickers. She strokes my arm, and talks on and on.

The garden is a drove of flowering trees. There are Christmas decorations hanging in one of them. As I look at them, the shining baubles and the star moving about in the breeze, I feel a shower of sparks gathering inside my brain. I try to focus on my mother's hand, soft on my arm, keeping me here on the ground. But my arm doesn't feel part of me. It feels like some weird, fleshy plant, my hand its decoration.

We go to Pelorus Bridge that afternoon. I'm determined to swim this time. Last time we were at Pelorus, I was too self-conscious to swim, so I stayed on the rocks and batted sandflies while my brothers dived off a high rock. They created explosive splashes, then they burst upward, their faces a rictus of cold as the current swept them downstream. There's a photograph of me in that water as a girl, post-jump, holding my head above the surface, mouth open wide. I remember how cold it was. The audacity of the water to be so cold.

From the rocks below, I wait for the jumpers. Before long, two of them run along the bridge to the midpoint, climb over the railing, and hold themselves there for a few seconds. You can see them realizing that it's too late to back out now. Everyone is watching. There is a large sign that warns against jumping, but no one takes any notice of it. They look down, plotting their entry point. Then they launch, pumping their arms and legs and howling as they fall toward the water. Involuntarily I picture them falling onto rocks, turning white and gray and red, obliterated into nothingness. But the sound of watery impact carries across the river like a gunshot. Finally their heads surface and their arms shoot out of the water, pumping the air.

If this were fiction, what would happen is that on Christmas Day the girl would strip off and jump into the water. The cold would make her shriek and she would become aware of every cell of her body. The plunge into water is like *ardha kurmasana*, the most rejuvenating Bikram posture, in which your head hangs below your heart so that high-speed blood floods your face, bathes your brain. Of course the river would represent the constant, torrenting flux and change of life itself, and the girl's plunge would represent a rebirth, a kind of baptism. Fully submerged, she would realize, and the reader too, that she had been mistaken all along: it isn't possible to transform oneself despite all of her efforts; that indeed by trying to do so she is missing out on experiences that might make her a good person, and this realization is in itself a transformation, the best kind, one of those capsule moments in which we are conscious of growing up, growing stronger. The girl would realize this. The reader would witness a healing. Both would be carried downstream.

At last, a person can only attempt to describe. All symbols are imaginary, all explanation is unreal. There are only ever small ripples of change, and they move so slowly we can't feel them moving; or we tell ourselves that change is happening, but it is happening outside of us. We fine-tune ourselves like antennae, only to find the signal gone and static pouring into us. Even as we give ourselves over to them, we eventually give up the postures that claim our body as a perfect stage. When I take my breath and jump into the space between the rock and the coldest water, I become light as air. I am air, and I try to stay like this, suspended, made whole in air, in stillness. But my feet hit the water and I go down.

unveiling

I'm going to Feilding, a town in the lower North Island, for a couple of days with my friend Russell. Russell is a freelance photographer who, a few years ago, moved here from South Africa with his family. He is always looking to photograph people from small communities in New Zealand, and through a friend, he's heard the story of a family he wants to shoot. He's asked me to write something about them, and although I'm not a journalist, and although the only person I will know there is Russell, I've said yes.

The family are gathering for a man named Paul, who died last year after surgery to replace two of his heart valves. Paul was in his early forties and had worked as a bodyguard and a bouncer. He left behind a daughter, four brothers, and his parents, in their sixties. And now, one year after his funeral, it's time for the unveiling, the Māori ceremony in which the cloth covering Paul's headstone is drawn away. The unveiling is meant to signal that it's time for his family and friends to move forward. And this is the occasion that Russell and I will record.

On the drive up from Wellington, Russell tells me about a man called Michael he'd recently photographed standing in a small patch of vegetation between Five Mile Bay and the Taupo Airport. Michael was an expert skydiver. A few years earlier, he had been doing a fairly routine jump with a friend at Lake Taupo, jumping from the plane at around twelve thousand feet. When he tried to deploy his parachute, it didn't work: he looked up and saw it twisted above him, refusing to release. He tried to deploy the emergency parachute, but that didn't open either. At that point he started spinning around and around as he fell—he had a camera attached to his helmet, so there is footage in which you can see the spinning and hear Michael's voice. He realized he was going to die, so he said good-bye. As he fell he thought about trying to steer himself toward the lake, but he was falling too fast and was nearing blackout from the force. His father was a police surgeon and had told him what happened to people in high-impact accidents, so he knew exactly what would happen to him. His fall became one long, horrible bracing for impact. But instead of concrete or grass, what caught him was a six-foot-high thicket of blackberry. The thicket was like a fat thorny mattress.

He crashed through it in a tangle of parachute lines. He was still conscious when his friend, who had landed safely with his parachute, reached him—but then he blacked out. He had a punctured lung and a broken ankle, Russell tells me, and his body made a dent in the vegetation that lasted for months.

A marae is a sacred meeting place for Māori. A simple open area in front of the communal meetinghouse known as the wharenui, the marae is the place where traditional customs are carried out according to Māori protocol: formal meetings, funerals, celebrations, weddings, tribal reunions. The marae embodies the Māori proverb:

> *He aha te mea nui o te ao? He tāngata, he tāngata, he tāngata!*
>
> What is the most important thing in the world? It is the people, it is the people, it is the people!

There's a tree on the marae that's filled with kids. It's one of those trees that seem to have multiple trunks, with long grass and flowers growing in the middle of it, so kids can play in its base before clambering up into the spangly branches. The whole tree is lurching crazily. Kids carry other kids. A couple of kids carry babies. The babies look unfazed at being carried up into the tree by people only a bit taller than them. One kid carries a tiny radio that plays scratchy music from out of the tree. The kid leaps from branch to branch. The poor tree is losing it. Down on the lawn, the adults sit around talking and shouting and smoking. "That's a good tree, isn't it," says one of the elders, when he sees me watching. "Been there for I don't know how long. Friendly tree."

On a marae very few people will ask who you are or what you are doing there, even someone like me, who is walking around uncertainly, just looking, and sometimes scribbling something in my notebook. I have been hongied and kissed a lot. Whenever I see someone I haven't met yet, he or she comes up to greet me. I haven't done this kind of intensive greeting in years, and the first time, when we're all lined up on the Friday afternoon, I get confused and move the wrong way and end up kissing an elder on the lips. He doesn't flinch. Even a rooster that the kids find down by the river ("Go down to the river, come back with a rooster!") and bring back to the marae seems unfazed. It sits in the arms of a young boy, chortling quietly, as the kids fuss over it.

One of Paul's younger brothers, Rangi, has seen me writing in my notebook. He wants me to write a story about his sexual exploits. "Call it 'Rangi's Conquests'!" He and two others tell me a story about when the teenage Rangi tricked his parents into thinking he was going eeling at night but he was really going out to kiss girls. I then get into a long conversation with an old friend of Paul's, Bruce, who has a walrus moustache and slightly unfocused but bright blue eyes. He tells me about how much he is looking forward to the ham tournament that year. I ask what a ham tournament is. "Well," Bruce says, "it's a golf tournament where if you win you get a ham. Ham tournament, that's right." He's nodding as if he hasn't registered my ignorance, as if he is asked such questions all the time.

When I ask Bruce about Paul, he says, "A big man. He had the personality of a big man. He looked bulletproof." He remembers Paul weightlifting to make himself bigger for his work in security. About a year and a half before Paul died, he was in jail for assault. There, his size was a blessing, as it kept people away from him. But it was also harming him: the weightlifting made his heart valves leak, and the rheumatic fever that he'd had as a child flared up again.

"He never really looked after himself, even toward the end," one of Paul's brothers, Trevor, tells me. "He was told to give himself a better chance, and the fact was, he didn't have the motivation to do that. He was reckless. And there are some big gaps. It was difficult to know fully what Paul was up to."

Trevor is a fit, leather-jacketed man in his forties. Of the five brothers, he is the one who has most visibly made a different life for himself. In his early twenties he competed in boxing at the Barcelona Olympic Games, and won bronze at the 1994 Commonwealth Games in Victoria. He's now a member of the New Zealand Order of Merit for services to sports and community. As a kind of outsider now, he has a clear perspective on his family. "Our family aren't strongly immersed in Māori culture," he says. "It's only really since Paul's death that we've been more connected to the marae. Mum and Dad were part of that generation who thought that being Māori wasn't necessarily helpful for getting a job in a Pākehā world. So it was never really encouraged when we were kids." When the boys were teenagers, Paul's parents applied for a contract with social welfare to run a family home—a place where they could foster children who could no longer live with their parents. So the family moved to a large house. "We'd have fifteen people for dinner," says Trevor. "People would come to drop off kids who'd been taken off their parents."

As a teenager, Paul was prescribed monthly injections of penicillin to control his rheumatic fever, but he always slipped away when it came time to go to the school nurse. He left school when he was fifteen, and when he was seventeen, he stabbed a man and went to jail for four years. When he was released, his parents bought him a one-way ticket to England for his twenty-first birthday. He went to London, where he stayed for four years—overstaying his visa—working as a bouncer and bodyguard. Trevor tells me that he made a name for himself there. He was a lot more worldly after being away, and being back in Palmerston North was a downer.

When Paul was last in jail, he wrote to Trevor asking for money so that he could fix up his car. Trevor gave him the money and Paul got it fixed. When Paul died, Trevor ended up with the car. He sold it, and the money went toward Paul's headstone.

Naomi, eight, is one of Paul's nieces. She has an asymmetrical haircut and a toothache. "Mum keeps forgetting to ring the dentist." She swings between laughter and wholehearted misery because of her sore tooth. When I'm in the wharenui, writing in my notebook because I feel too shy to keep talking to everyone, she sits next to me. My mattress is right next to Paul's bed—there is a photo of him in a frame propped against a pillow on an empty mattress, a custom to show where he would sleep if he were here. A heavyset man with a gentle face, a dark tattoo on his shoulder. Naomi strokes the photo and says, "Hello Paul." Then she asks me to sing something, and we battle about this for what feels like twenty minutes. "Auē, please! I'll sing if you sing. What if we go over to that corner where no one can hear?" "No, I just really don't want to sing. I only sing when there's no one around." "But what if I block my ears?" "Then there's no point." "What if you sing some Miley Cyrus? I don't know what it's called, but that song. I really like that song." "I don't like Miley Cyrus that much. You can sing that song, though, if you want, and I'll listen." She starts half laughing, half singing, then buries her head in a pillow. "I can't do it!" This conversation is repeated several times. When I sit down outside the wharenui to put on my shoes again, she sits next to me. "Do those shoes really fit your feet?" She hugs me. "You're warm, have you been sitting in the sun?"

I have been. There is a lot of sitting and standing around at the marae, in the sun, in a big group. Doing not very much for a long time with a lot of people—which should be relatively easy—feels like using a muscle I've forgotten, like staggering around with a dead leg hoping no one will notice. I think about the kids in the tree, clambering around shouting at one another, and how much better they are at being among people than I am.

Russell is good at being on the marae. He has that photographer's knack of fully occupying his role, and so he seems to fit even as he is on the edge of a scene. With his camera on a strap around his neck, he has a look of relaxed authority. "You'll need a new neck!" a woman says to him, and there are shouts of

"Yeah, a new neck!" Russell gives a crowd-pleasing grin and lopes off, raising his camera to the tree on the lawn.

Bunnythorpe Cemetery is freshly mowed. It looks as if the ground has been swept completely smooth, planed in a way that suggests the curve of the earth, with the headstones bolting it in place. Some of the gravestones are busy with decoration: toy bumblebees and butterflies, spinning wheels, spinning flowers. The cemetery is almost empty today except for the crowd who have gathered, their cars parked not far away, at Paul's grave for the unveiling of his headstone. The stone is covered in two cloths—a soft black cloth, and over it, a mat woven with feathers. Paul's father and Paul's daughter, Lillee, pull them away. The headstone beneath is gray marble. Pressed into it is a photograph of Paul, dark-eyed, unsmiling, the same portrait as the one leaning against the pillow on Paul's symbolic bed.

Someone sings "Amazing Grace." There is a cold persistent breeze; the pinwheels on graves are spinning fast. Paul's parents hold hands, leaning on each other. A man named Blackie, who was Paul's teacher, speaks briefly about Paul and how strong and kind he was.

After the speeches and the singing, people stand around drinking from cups of homebrew and listening to "Proud Mary" from a car stereo. One of Paul's nieces, who is transgender, wears a black beanie over long wings of glossy black hair that she constantly strokes. Her face is pale with powder and she wears beautiful bright red lipstick. She sips from her cup and talks behind her hands to her friends. She gives me the thumbs-up when she sees me looking.

Back on the marae, the little kid who had the radio in the tree asks me where everyone went in their cars, and how come he got left behind. He's wearing red Speed Racer pajama pants and has bare feet. "We went up to the cemetery for the unveiling of Paul's headstone," I tell him. "Is that the cemetery at Bunnythorpe?" "Yes, that's the one." "Oh that's where my granddad's buried!" he tells me. "And my mum, my mum's buried there too." He runs off waving his radio.

I am sitting with Ben, one of the elders, under a corrugated iron shelter out the back of the kitchen. Above us is a row of dull metal hooks, where earlier, wild pigs have been hanging to be gutted. Ben is drinking Tui pale ale from a plastic cup—there's a chiller filled with it. "I seen you walking around with that note-book," he says, "and I thought to myself she must be writing something."

Ben has been going to exercise classes to help him with his breathing. He gave up smoking about sixteen years ago; before then he had smoked for most of his life. "You must be a lot better than you would've been if you'd kept smoking?" I say. He says, "Oh, no, I'm worse. It's the giving up that did it. The shock." But he says he's been a lot better since starting the exercise classes.

"Saint John's come and pick me up on Tuesdays and Thursdays and take me there and then they bring me home." He feels sorry for some of the other people there. Some of them are in wheel-chairs, some can't move around much, and some have worse emphysema than he does. "They say, 'Ben, why are you here? You're healthy as!' But it helps me a lot, so, I keep going." Ben would be in his seventies, I think. He wears blue sunglasses and a duffel coat, and he agrees with everything you say: "That's right, that's right." He used to be a jockey, then he got too heavy so he started sheep shearing.

Everywhere there is smoke. Smoke coming off the hāngī in white sheets just after they light it. Smoke pouring out of the portable fire inside a can near the shelter where we're sitting. And nearly everyone's smoking constantly, except Ben. They poke their cigarettes into the fire to light them. Between drags, the wind picks up the smoke trails. The smoke blows every-where: into the clean tea towels on the clothesline, into the men standing around the hāngī in gumboots, into Ben and me sitting on the bench under the pig hooks.

Ben tells me that everyone here has their placenta and umbil-ical cord buried in the land around the marae. One of his nieces was born in Perth but she had hers sent back in a Tupperware container and buried here. He says they're thinking about creat-ing a virtual marae—"marae in the sky!"—for people living overseas to visit online. Some people won't like the technology thing, though. "I can't even really use this bloody cellphone," says Ben, pulling a Nokia out of his pocket. "Stupid thing, don't even know how to answer it! Hello? Hello? Can't even turn it off!"

. . .

Paul's daughter, Lillee, is carrying around a big stuffed dog with matted fur and a weird pink mouth that flaps open and shut.

"What's his name?" asks Russell. Lillee says, "Russell."

Russell laughs. "He can't be called Russell. I'm Russell."

"He's Russell."

Later, a boy shows me the picture he's decided to get tattooed on his back one day. The design, on a sweatshirt, is a circle with swirls inside it, the logo for the club where he goes to learn jujitsu. Emblazoned underneath the logo is *Russell.*

After we lie down in the wharenui that night, I can't sleep except for one fragmented hour in the early morning (there's a party out the back of the kitchen that keeps going until around five in the morning, and also everyone in the wharenui is snoring, but Russell, next to me, is definitely the loudest and most persistent) and I swear, around midnight, I hear someone hissing: "Russ! Where's Russ?"

First thing in the morning, when I'm trying to figure out how to get unnoticed to the bathroom while blind, as I can't find my glasses, the kids are telling "yo momma" jokes. There's no laughter in between; they're just reciting the jokes like times tables, sometimes finishing the punch lines for one another before moving on to the next one. They don't direct the lines at anyone in particular. It's as if there's one ubiquitous mum out there, struggling away through her daily routines. "Your mum's so fat she makes a beeping noise when she's reversing."

"Your mum's so fat she sat on a TV and it turned into a flat-screen TV."

Someone takes personal offense. "Auē, so? Least she's got a flat-screen TV."

"Your mum's so fat she was lying on the beach and Greenpeace tried to push her back in the sea. 'Cause . . . they thought she was a whale."

Some of the kids are sniggering now. "A whale! That's a stink joke, eh. A *whale*."

"There was an opportunity around Paul dying," Trevor will tell me later. "That it would engender a different kind of cohesiveness for the family, that we would do more together. But it was short-lived. We're back to where we used to be. We've moved on."

But for now, at the marae, Russell has everyone—the elders, the kids, the cooks, the brothers, the in-laws, everyone—stand or sit in front of the marae in the shade of its awning, to take one group portrait. I stand off to one side. The kids do bunny ears and rapper poses. There are maybe seventy people crammed together, and we're all waiting for the sun to dim so that Russell can take the picture. "Once it goes behind the cloud," he shouts, "we only have a few seconds to take the photo, so be ready." There begins a commentary on what the sun is doing and how long it will take to go. "Is it going? It must be nearly behind the cloud." "Stupid sun! Fuckin' get behind that cloud!" After a few minutes of this, the light seems to ebb. The voices rise, encouraging it. I look up and the sun is moving through a thin blanket of cloud. A roar goes up. "The sun's going in the cloud!" The sun finally reaches a thicker part of the blanket, and shade briefly falls over the marae. Everyone roars again. Russell takes the photo, and he manages about three more before the sun comes out again and the group erupts out onto the lawn, into the sun, into the tree. In the photograph, the tekoteko at the peak of the wharenui seems to break the clouds in two.

on breathing

I have decided to begin breathing noisily again when I am puffed, rather than trying to conceal the breathing.

In the past, I must have decided that breathing noisily when puffed was a sign of weakness, and that anyone who noticed the noisy breathing would think, "That woman is unfit." I can't remember how or why I decided this, but it might have been something to do with climbing a mountain while on a school trip, and a boy was lagging up the mountain behind everyone else, breathing noisily, and hearing the person beside me mutter, "John is unfit." As we turned to watch, John crept very slowly toward us, crablike with his huge pack, his eyes lowered as he breathed noisily.

It might have been that, or it might have been something else, such as climbing some steps with my mother, or a combination of things.

For years now I have tried to quiet my breathing, when puffed, by letting the breath out thinly, like a slow leak from a puncture, or even pretending that it was a sigh, as if I had just remembered an important task. So whenever I was riding my bike up one of the many hills that I ride up each day, I tried not to move my mouth too much, because this would betray my noisy breathing. I also tried to maintain an unflustered, slightly bored expression, as if I were making so little effort that I could mentally absent myself from the scene. I didn't want to attract the attention of anyone walking along the road, especially not anyone who would recognize me and think, "Ashleigh Young is unfit." One of my bigger fears, and one I thought about every day, was that an old boyfriend of mine, who I know goes to the university, would be passing in a bus and look out the window and see me there at the roadside, breathing noisily. "She has got unfit," he would think to himself. I suppose this might still happen.

I am slightly puffed after walking the three flights of steps from my flat to the street with my bike over my shoulder. I am averagely puffed when I begin the climb toward the university. I am very puffed when I get to the top of the Terrace, and I am extremely puffed by the time I am creeping through the roundabout at the top of the street beside the university; I use a last bit of energy to throw my arm sideways to signal the turn. When I am locking up my bike, I am so puffed that it feels like my lungs have turned into a pair of excited dogs and they are jumping up and down, trying to feed on the air. My lungs paw and salivate at the air, tearing bits out of it like stuffing. By now I am defeated. Anyone who walks down the path behind me will see a woman untangling a bike lock while breathing not just noisily but extravagantly, on a breathing spree, and the thought will probably come to them, even just for a second before it is swept up by a stream of other thoughts: "That woman is unfit."

Sometimes I have been stuck behind slower-moving male cyclists who I could tell were breathing noisily, but I still have not been moved to allow myself to do the same.

Once I had a slow crash when a woman in a parked car opened her door into my path. But even that didn't remind me that there were more important things to worry about than my breathing.

Last week a couple of teenage boys shouted abuse at me when I was just at the steepest, most difficult part of the hill, and I didn't have enough air in my lungs to shout abuse back, but even that didn't make me think I should let myself breathe noisily, as required.

Today, nothing in particular happened to make me decide to breathe noisily again when I am puffed. So, just as I'm not sure why I decided that I had to breathe quietly, I am now not sure why I have decided that I don't have to. I pushed my bike through the gate and my cat, Jerry, immediately came running out from under a tree, screeching at me. He screeched loudly and continuously as he ran down the steps just in front of my feet. I leaned my bike against the fence and put its special bicycle raincoat on, which is always more difficult than I think it will be, like putting a pair of pants on a car. Then I came inside and lay down on the floor and breathed noisily until I was no longer puffed. All this time, Jerry was prancing around me, screeching for food and maybe, I hope, because he was glad to see me. Maybe it felt like enough time had passed and that I could breathe now.

on going away

J ust like in the story you have read, it's possible that the man does not mean the words; means the anger in them, yes, but not the words themselves. He has said the words many times, and each time you have gone away for a little while, then despite yourself you have come back and found that he is not angry anymore, that in fact he is glad to see you. On those occasions, saying "Go away" seems to give him comfort. Like giving someone flowers, the words make the present situation clear, return it to a simpler time of giving and receiving. Perhaps saying the words makes him feel that his life will be easier now. His life will have more room for other people now that you have gone away, it will have room for other people, other futures, even as a secret part of him hopes to see you again.

The man says it is final this time. But many other times it has been final. The exact composition of finality has become uncertain. You have gone away and come back so often that perhaps it is all that is true between the two of you now, the going away, the coming back. Perhaps without these surges of anger and relief, you would have simply drifted away, not being called out to, not being drawn back. It is also true that you enjoy the man not being angry anymore, and the relief of being beside him again, in that time when you say kind words to each other. It is a physical relief, like being on a long, turbulent flight and then finally crawling into a soft bed at the other end; how engrossing that night's sleep is, how fully it returns you to the ground.

On one or two occasions, you have stayed away, adopting a certain coldness each time you recalled the man's words. You have worked hard to remember the moment in which the words were said to you. On those occasions the coldness has simply lost its grip on you, like a new language you've learned turning back into gibberish. And on those occasions, after much time has passed and much struggling to sustain your bitterness, the man has said, "Come back," and, suddenly flooded with warmth, you have gone. But this time he has not. The words "go away" stay before you, and as the days pass, it seems that these words slowly settle and a truth grows around them.

You consider how your own circumstances might be different from the circumstances of a woman in a story. The woman in the story seems always to go back and the man in the story seems always to receive her. There is always at least one going back, the final one, that is more joyful than all the others.

But you, here now, could swiftly go away, and stay gone. You could keep going until enough time has passed for the man to fall from your thoughts and for you to fall from his, even as, at this moment, motionless, the book still in your hands, it doesn't seem possible. The man's thoughts and your own have grown together, just as the things you own have grown together, small possessions and pieces of clothing piling up steadily. However, maybe your love will stay whole and good if you go away only one more time, instead of many more times, since each time of going away adds another day to travel, another long flight to recover from—even as, at this moment, you wonder if the going away and the coming back have made you both stronger for each other, have made both your hearts wiry as greyhounds.

You consider how staying in one place and yet becoming silent is a form of going away. In our silence, as we lie beside each other in the moments before sleep, and wake up beside each other in the morning, the going away creeps out of us.

There must be a way to compress all the going away into a single moment. Even if the moment were horrible, it would still be only a moment. It would be like watching a driverless car roll down a steep hill, or like stepping into a manhole. A sharp, pure accident with a beginning and an end. When it is over, you won't even be gone, but simply somewhere else. And the man—having now departed from the point at which he told you to go away—will be walking briskly. He will be smiling and holding the seat of a child's bicycle as he pushes it along. And after a little while he will look back on you fondly and without anger, and eventually you will grow very faint inside his past.

anemone

On a long-haul flight, time stretches, warps, balloons. As we fly across time zones, in and out of days and nights, time becomes a tangible substance that we move through, like dense fog, or like water. It seems to exist only in the space outside the plane. Inside the plane there is no real time, and there is no real sleep and no real waking. The air-conditioning circulates the same brittle air. People communicate in nudges and murmurs. We try to sleep, lopsided in our seats, like crushed cans. It's a strange static dimension—at first enjoyable, because there's nothing to do but read, eat, drink, and sit, and it feels like a little holiday, but soon those actions begin to wear and we long to walk into another room and talk to somebody or open a door and walk outside. On this flight, between Auckland and Los Angeles before flying on to London, I was sitting next to two young rugby players in their uniforms, and I was reading Alan Lightman's book *The Accidental Universe*. It's a collection of essays in which—very broadly—Lightman, a physicist, explores discoveries about the universe from a philosophical and emotional perspective as well as a scientific one. It's a book I've read before, but I was reading it differently this time, paying closer attention, hoping that my semi-wakefulness might lower my defenses and help me notice more. Lightman is an unusual physicist in that he's intensely interested in religion—particularly Buddhism—and literature and art, and in how these things widen a scientific perspective, and vice versa. He has that kind of restless, search-beaming mind that, as you follow it, seems to open up possibilities for understanding the universe, and the tiny accidental blip of human life within it, even as he arrives at more questions rather than answers. Reading this book reminds me of my first memories of flying in a plane, with my parents and my brothers, JP and Neil—looking out the window and down at the town below, seeing the cars on the tiny roads, the rivers, the sheep. I was thrilled and haunted by how small all our busyness had become.

On my flight I read one of the essays, "The Temporary Universe," a number of times. There was something in it that I wanted to grasp but couldn't. It opens with Lightman describing his daughter's wedding, and his feeling that it's a sort of tragedy—

he wishes that she could have stayed the same, that he could have his younger daughter back, as she was at ten or twenty. (She's only thirty in this essay, but all right, fair enough, Lightman.) He has this irrational wish, he explains, for permanence, despite his scientific understanding that everything around us—the universe, the earth, our own bodies—is relentlessly shifting and evaporating. Nature shows us that time is constantly wearing away at what we know in this moment, and that to hope for lasting stability is futile. But in a profound contradiction, people still cling: to knackered old shoes, to photographs, to products that might make us look more like our younger selves, to a house perched on a cliff top that's falling into the sea. This clinging is ridiculous in the face of the second law of thermodynamics—otherwise known as the arrow of time—and yet many of us can't relinquish our desire that the people and the things that we love should never change and never leave us. "The universe has an infinite supply of time and can outlast any player," says Lightman. I was expecting him to leave it there: to tell us with a shrug and a smile, like the cobbler who can't fix your falling-apart shoes anymore, that we have to accept this and get on with things. But then he suggests that, maybe, nature is not yet complete. Maybe it's nature, not us, that can be found wanting. "Perhaps this immortal thing that we wish for exists beyond time and space."

A few short days earlier, my brother Neil's partner of nearly ten years, the mother of their two small children, Kiwa and Ngaire, took her own life. When I spoke to Neil on the day that it happened, a Saturday morning on the other side of the world, when paramedics and police were still in his home in Brixton,

I heard a roaring sound in my ears and my whole body seemed to go numb. Then it felt like time stopped. The next morning, when it was night in London and the end of Neil's first day living with what had happened, I walked outside. I saw a young woman pushing a pram with a toddler inside it, and a dog on a leash trotting beside them. A few cars hissed past, and a cyclist. These were indications that time was continuing to continue. Each indication felt piercing, acute, like the harshest glare of sunlight.

Neil was the one who found Jeng on the morning she died. On the first few days afterward, in deep trauma, when numbness set in, he said that he became like a sea anemone, responding only to the environment around him in each moment. I keep picturing a sea anemone, attached to the sea bottom, its skeletonless body triggered by the slightest touch. Beneath the weight of miles of water above it, it moves around very slowly in the dark.

Lightman quickly—but with empathy, letting us down gently—dismisses the notion that a magnificent immortal substance exists in nature. It's too preposterous to believe. And yet, like so many of us, he can't force his mind to the dark place where he might truly accept that "in a few short years, my atoms will be scattered in wind and soil, my mind and thoughts gone, my pleasures and joys vanished." In the essay's uplifting final paragraphs, he writes that perhaps mortality grants a sort of grandeur of its own; perhaps there is something majestic in the brevity of our lives. And he writes, of course, about the night-blooming cereus, the leathery plant that blooms for only one night a year.

It is very hard to see the grandeur of brevity when a person's life is cut short, and perhaps particularly hard when it is the person herself who cuts it short. Instead of beauty, the far stronger impression is of cruelty. When Lightman writes so vividly of the wearing effects of time, I think instead of the wearing effects of depression, with bitterness, because, while time outlasts us all, it's not inevitable that depression will outlast the depressive. When he writes of the way the universe falls apart and constantly yields to disorder, and the way that the genes of some living things are subjected to random chemical storms so that, in time, they become degraded, like "forks with missing tines," I think of these processes as the turmoil of depression, of what happened to Jeng in a space where nobody else could reach. In one way, this kind of thinking helps: Jeng was ill, and what happened may have been the result of a random storm of her illness, or perhaps the storm had been building for some time. In another way, it does not: if only she could have held on through this last storm. At this moment, the wish to reach into the past and hold on to someone is an even more profound futility than the futility of trying to stop time.

My seven-year-old nephew, Kiwa, likes to play Minecraft. The other day, Neil says, Kiwa found himself stuck inside a dimension of Minecraft that he couldn't get out of. He felt very alarmed by this and Neil had to help get him out of there, though it took some time and some trial and error. The FAQ boards providing advice on how to escape such dimensions say things like: "You need to set up a temporary shop by collecting leather, feather and sugarcanes, and go myst-hopping forth and back until you find one with a star fissure symbol. Temporary home, if you will." "Create a portal to the twilight forest. Once on the other side, if you jump through the portal to go back home, it seems to drop you in the overworld." "Die, then escape limbo by finding the void."

Maybe the place where his mum has gone, he said to Neil, is like the dimension in Minecraft. She has got lost, got stuck.

When I walked through Brixton the morning after I landed, on my way to Neil's, through the morning rush to the Tube, nearly every face I saw was squinting, grimacing, into bright gray sunlight, pressing forward.

I don't believe that we can ever consider the brevity of Jeng's life to be in itself beautiful, to be majestic. Just over a week later, accepting that she is no longer here and will not come back, is to force our minds into a dark place. Coming to terms with the inevitability of the past rather than of the future is the impossible thing; learning to live in the reality that one terrible decision has made seems like the impossible thing. But we can consider many, many moments of her life to be beautiful, each of these accidental, shining blips within a life, within a universe: Jeng walking through the Brixton markets with shopping bags over her shoulder, Jeng riding her bike to work, Jeng making dumplings, Jeng in the countryside holding Ngaire's hand. We can also consider the pressing forward of those left behind to be beautiful. As my brother paces himself through the coming days, not only trying to process a deep trauma but also working his way through many grim administrative tasks, such as speaking to a coroner and closing bank accounts and explaining to many people what has happened, he moves around a little bit more, begins to make the very first movements, very slowly, upward through the weight.

lark

"Julia, you should write a book," Graham says. Graham is a writer. He has done books about the Beatles, rugby, steam trains, and being a stay-at-home dad. This last one is our favorite; it is called *Just You Wait Till Your Mother Gets Home* and we recognize his daughters, our friends, in it; they are famous. Not all of the books have received good reviews, some have received very bad reviews, but Graham always has an advance on the way from his publisher. He tells my mother that he will help. They will sit down together over glasses of wine and the computer, and they'll get all the stories down. If she doesn't write them down they will be lost. That's one thing that you can count on in this life. Don't count on anyone else to remember anything; they'll remember it wrong or they'll remember it mercilessly. She must write it all down before it's too late. She doesn't need to use a pseudonym but might consider changing some names here and there.

Excited, she starts making notes at night after she's done her Japanese. Each night the desk lamp glows from the window of the caravan in the field. The caravan, an old brown-and-white trailer that its former owner once towed up and down the country on camping trips, is her study. She sits at the flimsy table in there with a blanket on her knees, reading or writing. We wait for the book. Our mother, who rode her bike alongside ours to school, even though she was nervous on the road; who stripped old chairs of paint and varnished them; who used a jackhammer to demolish broken concrete so she could lay new paving stones; who filled the bare garden of our new house with roses and hebes. In our mind we design the cover. It will have a black-and-white photograph of Julia—note that in the book she is known as Julia, not our mother, because in book form she is independent, childless, and glamorous—and the photograph shows her wearing goggles and a white scarf. She is long and thin like Amelia Earhart, standing beside a glider preparing to go solo; in the back of our mind we know that no such photograph exists but that doesn't particularly matter, because it is a book. It is a book of the stories she has told us and other hazy episodes that we suppose are not quite true but cannot relinquish from the picture of her. There is a whole album of photographs we've never seen but that we know well, as if we had grown up with them looking down from the piano lid, where all other photos are displayed: an uncle with his guitar and white cowboy hat somewhere in Niagara, another uncle and an auntie on a luxury cruise. There are people we have never met but we would know their faces if we saw them in the street. All of their stories will be in the book by our mother, but mostly the stories will be of her.

She was cycling home from the dentist's house when a glider appeared above her. It can't have been higher than a few feet above her head. She screamed, ducked, wobbled into the grass verge. She was a university student, and her long career of falling over had just begun. The glider was long-winged, like a diving heron; it was coming in to land at the Wigram airbase. She righted herself and stood still, shading her eyes, heart jumping. She'd felt the glider's slipstream and its shadow, rippling like a tree. After a minute or two her heart was calm and she got back on her bicycle and pedaled feebly toward England Street.

Soon she would get a motorbike, red, only 49 cc, but much faster than her stringy ten-speed, which frequently shucked off its chain. She had saved nearly enough money to park the bike in a shed forever.

They shared the cooking at Julia's flat. Margaret cooked simple, bland dinners that they ate quickly in front of the television.

Julia tried to mimic her mother's pies of gravy, pastry, thick-cut carrots and parsnips, steak and kidney. The pies were substantial—"filling," as her father always said when praising her mother's pies, as if all one could ask of food was that it piled up in the stomach—but their flavor was the same as their color: a thick brown. When Julia's other flatmate, Mary, did the cooking she took hours. She boiled everything. The food, finally served at ten p.m., was inedible. Every vegetable had been boiled into oblivion, except—by some cruel twist—the potatoes, which were hard as fresh pears. There were a few forlorn chops, or a pool of ground meat. And Mary burned the bottom of Julia's special cooking pot, the one Julia's mother had given her. "You be sure to feed yourself properly," she'd said, and along with the pot, she gave Julia a bag of freshly dug potatoes and a packet of saveloys, which Mary had promptly boiled to death, splitting their skins open.

Julia ate chocolate bars from the dairy. Sometimes her mother would send a tin of baking from Oamaru, and she would eat from this too as she lay on the bed with her French assignments. Tan square, shortbread, Louise cake—she ate slowly, tasting the warm kitchen and the cracked plates. Banana cake and Turkish delight in a cold Agee jar, Anzac biscuits. When she looked up from her textbook she was sometimes annoyed to find herself alone in the chilly room in England Street.

Her father hadn't wanted her to go to university. On her last night at home he'd poured whiskey after whiskey. "So you're off to get the BA," he chuckled, "and we all know what that stands for." He took another swig. "Bugger all!" He thumped the table and wheezed with laughter. Her mother tied on her apron and said, "Oh, Doug."

At home for a weekend, one morning she was lying in bed, dozing, happy in a half-awake way that she was not at England Street. She heard her mother tiptoe in, then tiptoe out. Then she heard her mother whispering to her father in the kitchen, where they were having breakfast. "Gosh, she's big, Doug," her mother said, "she's got so big."

Julia opened her eyes. She felt the old bed sag. She stayed in bed for another hour. Tears ran into her ears. When she couldn't hear her parents anymore, she got up. On her way out she glanced evilly at the mirror, at her nightie shape. She couldn't imagine looking at the mirror with warmth or curiosity ever again. She felt embarrassed by all the times when she had. These things should have made it easy to leave.

On Fridays in Christchurch she dressed in old clothes and cycled to her cleaning job. The dentist owned the house, and it was vast, really an open mouth of a house, and she sometimes found herself thinking the same thing she imagined the dentist himself thinking in his line of work: *Some people really are filthy.* Her work took at least five hours. To be fair, it wasn't that the dentist and his wife were dirty. They just didn't see dirt where Julia did. It was like being color-blind or having no sense of smell. They didn't see that the light switches were coated in a kind of plaque or that the toastie-pie maker crouched in a puddle of its own filth. Every morning the sun streamed through the brownish mesh curtains and ripened everything in the kitchen; it smelled of sweetly rotting fruit: bananas, pears, large pithy lemons from the tree. Under her feet, the linoleum was bulgy. Damp got into everything. Always the house was as quiet as an empty school hall, and she tried to be quiet, too, and to work quickly; she didn't quite believe that no one was hiding, watching her. She half imagined a secret room behind one of the paintings on the wall, where a watcher could look through the eyes of a person in the painting, like in a horror movie.

She had been instructed not to touch the piles of books and photographs on the desk in the living room: she must work around them. Neither was she to touch the fancy teacups, beer steins, and wooden ornaments that crowded every surface. Once, she picked up an Aboriginal figurine by its head, intending to dust behind it. A little wooden thing unfolded from the figurine's flax skirt: a penis. Julia dropped the figurine. It fell back on the piano lid, upsetting the other figurines. She scrambled to reposition them—they had been assembled in a group as if in earnest conversation—then walked quickly away from the yellow-toothed piano.

The bedroom was the worst. She changed the dentist's sheets as quickly as possible, feeling like a thief. The bed lay in the middle of the room covered in swaths of sheets and blankets. With a flicker of dread, she pushed them back. She suspected that one day she would find someone curled up underneath.

Surprise! He would grin and reach for her.

The dentist left the money in a brown envelope behind the toaster: two dollars. Years later her husband, too, would leave her a weekly allowance in a brown envelope. Neither the dentist nor her husband ever spoke of the money as anything other than the brown envelope. "I will leave the brown envelope behind the toaster," the dentist would say. "I'll bring the brown envelope home," her husband would later say. The sight of the envelope stirred up the same feelings in her: first relief, then a creeping discomfort, an urge to account for herself. And then, when she opened the envelope, relief again.

At first she answered the ad simply to get out of the house. *Learn to Glide.* She also remembered the white bird, the glider that had toppled her off the road. She looked around the England Street flat; she thought of her French assignments; she thought of last night's meal. What else could she do? She called the number. How easy it was to be officially learning to do something. She'd called the number, and now, even as she stood in the tepid kitchen, she could tell people, "I am learning to glide." As if gliding were just a new kind of sewing technique. She knew her father would be appalled, would stride around the kitchen huffing.

On Sunday, and every Sunday after that, she rode out to the Wigram airbase on her 49 cc. Her mother was right, she had gotten big, and the motorbike was too small for her; she could feel its wheels pressing too firmly into the road. Still, it was more dignified than the bicycle, which was now sagging against a pole on the back porch.

At Wigram there was nothing but a hut-like office and a parking lot. And the airfield, of course, but the airfield itself was nothing, only a flatness. The sky came all the way down to the ground, so that even the ground—prickly and sparse—looked unsure of itself; its sole purpose, really, was to push things upward so they could get into the sky.

The gliding instructor shook her hand. His name was Andy. He didn't seem at all surprised that a young woman wanted gliding lessons. "It's twenty dollars per hour of towing time," he told her, "but on your first flight we won't be up there for an hour, more like forty minutes, just so's you see what it's like inside. For the first flight you'll be in the backseat. After that you'll be in the front. I'll be guiding you from the back." He explained that the towing plane—a Tiger Moth—would take them up. It would tow them along above Canterbury, and at approximately two thousand feet Andy would drop the tow rope, severing the Lark from the Tiger Moth. The Tiger Moth would fly away and the Lark would gradually lose height. Andy would carefully steer it back toward the airbase, and come in to land on the strip.

The Lark was a skinny, cigar-shaped thing—not quite a plane, not quite a kite—with a long front window and a pointed nose. It was Czech. It had no propeller, which made it seem more vulnerable than an ordinary aircraft. Its wings were so far outstretched they looked cartoonish; all the glider needed was eyes and a goofy grin painted on its fuselage. The wings were detachable—they could be unclipped and folded up so that the wingless glider became like a tadpole. Then it could be easily stored in a shed.

Andy smiled at her, a freckled man with advancing jowls. He looked so soft and faded with graying hair, his crumpled shorts and polo shirt. "Ready?" He opened the door of the Lark.

At takeoff, the Tiger Moth pulled them promptly along the runway. The Lark skittered along on the end of the rope, bumping and bobbing on its hard, hoof-like wheels, as if it were galloping, and then the Tiger Moth rose up ahead of them, a silver insect in the window, and the ground came unstuck and fell away. They rose in the air, at first swaying pendulously, slowly becoming level. She became aware of her weight and her eyes in a way she had never been on the ground—how every movement altered the Lark's bearing.

Over the next few months, Andy taught her that the little half-moon on the dashboard must always be level. He taught her to steer using the controls, which looked a little like metal hooks on a man's arms, and to keep straight, to *glide*, not lurch about as if she were on a bike. It was cramped inside the Lark. Her legs were not able to stretch all the way out and she was aware of the roof only a few centimeters above her hair. She was also aware of Andy in the backseat, watching carefully as she held the controls. The aircraft smelled like cracked vinyl and stale nicotine, engine oil and aftershave.

She'd thought it would be silent to glide. Instead there was a whining, groaning noise. It was the Lark's motor, a halfhearted motor that did not particularly want to be in the air, would perhaps have been more at home in a lawnmower. Despite this,

Julia wasn't scared. She was afraid of heights—even looking up at tall buildings gave her vertigo; she had to clutch on to something—but in the sky it was different because the land was too far away to trigger any fear. From this distance, land was an abstraction, as clouds were from the ground; Christchurch was carved flat, a postoperative land, sewn up in green and brown and yellow. Being apart from it was a relief.

At about two thousand feet she would press the lever that released the tow rope. There was a loud *whoomph* and then, finally, there was silence. This meant the motor had cut out and they were alone and motorless in the air. The first time this happened, Julia looked back at Andy and he gave her the thumbs-up. His pink face was sandwiched between thick black earmuffs. Were they lawn-mowing earmuffs? She turned back and held on to the controls. She was above Canterbury, gradually losing height. During this descent, she always felt a mixture of dread and glee in equal measure: gravitating toward something she wasn't sure she wanted to gravitate toward, but glad to be able to steer to get there, to be graceful and long-winged in her descent.

Once, the Tiger Moth ascended too quickly in front of them. The tow rope whipped up and snaked in the air and then dropped straight down behind the plane. Snap. The rope had snapped! There was silence, into which Julia screamed. "It's all right, it's all right," insisted Andy. He was right. She did not die. She did not crash into a mountain. Why would she? Nothing happened, just as Andy said it wouldn't. It was a clear day. She was at fourteen hundred feet, high enough to glide back to the airbase. Down she went through the layers of the sky, toward the earth, as if her eyes themselves were shedding layers, and her heart too, slowly shedding panic and becoming calm.

To land, she had to glide very low over roads and trees. It was here that the fear began to come back, because she could see the hard angles of the earth's surface. She could see roads and rooftops, cars and sheep; it was all too easy to imagine falling and impaling the Lark's body on one of its own wings. If any young women were cycling along the road, now was when she would make them topple sideways. But there was never a cycling woman, or any person, not that she could see. The road was always empty, as though no woman had ever been there at all.

Then one day Andy flew straight into the side of a mountain. She heard about it a few days after it happened. They said it was an unusually still day, hardly any wind but thick with fog, the day he died.

Years later she was in the air again, but this time she was gripping the back of a seat, her husband's seat—he was flying them through mountains over Alexandra and there was a storm coming up to meet them. Rain was hitting the windshield; each drop exploded like a bug. It was true that the closer you were to clouds the bigger the rain was, and when you were *inside* clouds the rain was obscene. They pitched from side to side, jolted violently up and down; their seat belts bit into their hips, and at one point their heads bumped the ceiling and she felt her stomach leap into her mouth, then fall through the floor. She started to think, *This could be it.* They would die up there in the mountains, like in a movie.

"Russell," she called, her voice bee-like in the roaring plane, but he didn't turn around. He was holding the controls and peering through the windshield into the white. He'd turned on the windshield wipers, and the mechanized arms butted frantically back and forth; even in the middle of it all she found this funny, as if they were in a flying car. The back of her husband's neck looked tense and purposeful. Also, it was speckled with worrying-looking moles she hadn't noticed before now. A person becomes hyperalert in a small aircraft flying in a storm.

On either side of her were children, one of whom was crying, the other of whom was staring out the window at the clouds racing greedily past on either side of them. She hung on to the back of the seat and prayed. Her husband flew, and the storm towed them through the mountains.

Her nails are ringed with dirt from the garden. Fine, wheat-colored hair grows on the backs of the hands. Beneath, veins have come to the surface. There are livery patches here and there: old burns from ovens and potbelly stoves. Our mother's skin is thinner, her veins looser and bluer, than ours. But we are old enough now that when her hand and ours are next to each other, they look as if they might belong to the same person. She has a new job cleaning a motel. She is telling us about it while we sit on the ground beside her garden table.

"I'm devoting myself to the metaphysical task of cleaning a mirror," she says, "wiping away every last trace of every person who has ever looked into that mirror." We are not sure what she means by metaphysical and suspect that she doesn't quite know either. She has a way of using words for her own ends. Now she takes a breath, eager to turn this idea into sense. "I'm trying to polish away every last breath and *pose* of anyone who has ever looked into that mirror, including the person who is looking into it right now. It's an almost impossible feat to make a mirror entirely spotless. You have to know what it means for a surface to have utter—clarity." She taps the table where she is sitting, making her fingers into a pecking beak. She does this often, for emphasis. "So I just stand back and look and hope for the best. And I think I'm getting a bit closer every day." She takes a sip of Riesling and fixes her gaze on the garden. We picture her appraising the mirror, poised with a cloth. Her hands are strong and soft. She wraps them around our wrists and pulls us up off the ground when we hold our arms out.

In the caravan she has taken down the Batman posters and put up kanji and hiragana charts. Above the sink she has Blu Tacked postcards of Japan and France. She has stacked textbooks on the bunks and folded up the folding bed. She has laid a sheepskin rug on a seat so that the dog can lie alongside her as she studies or writes. She has a tape recorder that plays a man saying the

Japanese vowel sounds, among other sounds. His voice is like a funny bird in the trailer. *Ka—ke—ki—ko—ku,* he says, then he pauses so Julia can say it back.

The caravan is slumped in the grass, parked in a field under a huge tree that drops moldering walnuts on the roof. Whenever Julia forgets to close the door, in the morning we find droppings on the carpet where one of the sheep has spent the night. The caravan smells like a closet full of heavy coats that won't be worn again. Soon it will have to be towed away and taken on holiday by the Man, a farmer who arrives in a truck and paces across the fields in sloppy gumboots and makes things disappear. He has taken our old sheep and our diseased and dying hens on holiday, presumably the same destination to which the caravan will one day go. The new hens bathe in the dirt under its rusting axles.

A wineglass with tidal marks is on the table beside Julia's father's desk lamp. The lamp is doubled over like something in pain. From our desk inside the house where we are studying, we can see her through the caravan's oblong window. Tonight she is at work on the book. She is trying to remember things. It is like practicing another sort of language. It leads her to herself and it leads her away. Sometimes it unsteadies her until she finds another small thread to hold on to. A moonish light comes from her window. Her cloudy head bends over the table as she writes.

acknowledgments

Thank you to all the people who helped me write this book and encouraged me so generously. I would have abandoned it otherwise. Thanks especially to Harry Ricketts and Chris Price, who helped me do the early groundwork, and to Fergus Barrowman for the patient, cheerful goading. I'm also very grateful to the International Institute of Modern Letters; Denis and Verna Adam; and the wonderful Michael Kelleher, Megan Eckerle, and the members of the committee who run the Windham-Campbell Literature Prizes at Yale University.

Thanks to the editors of the publications in which some of these pieces have previously appeared (in slightly different form), including *Landfall, Five Dials, Griffith Review, Sport,* and *Tell You What.*

Thank you, as ever, to the brilliant team at VUP, who have been so supportive. In the United States, thank you to Marya Spence for taking a gamble on me—I feel lucky to know you. To Cal Morgan, Jynne Martin, and the team at Riverhead Books, thank you for being so warm and welcoming to me.

And here at home, thank you to my co-teacher Rebecca Priestley. To Elliot for drawing Big Red in the storm. To Russell Kleyn, Trevor Shailer, and Kauwhata Marae. And to my close friends and family, especially Matt and my brothers, JP and Neil.

selected bibliography

"About Bikram Yoga." Yoga for the People. Accessed June 8, 2016. bikramyoga.co.nz/bikram-yoga-postures.aspx.

Allen, Pamela. *Black Dog*. Hawthorne, Australia: Penguin Books, 1992.

Bondeson, Jan. *A Cabinet of Medical Curiosities*. London and New York: W. W. Norton, 1999.

The Clampers. *Giant Diamond Eater*. 1999, compact disc.

"Clampers." H-townWiki. Last modified November 23, 2015. expdev.net/htownwiki/index.php/Clampers.

Eliade, Mircea. *Yoga: Immortality and Freedom*. Translated by Willard R. Trask. Princeton, NJ, and Oxford: Princeton University Press, 2009.

Evelyn, John. *The Diary of John Evelyn*. Edited by Guy de la Bédoyère. Woodbridge, England: Boydell Press, 2004.

"Ferdinand Cheval Known as Postman Cheval." Palais Idéal du Facteur Cheval. Accessed June 8. 2016. facteurcheval.com/en/history/postman.html.

"Ferdinand Cheval's Letter to André Lacroix." Palais Idéal du Facteur Cheval. Accessed June 8, 2016. facteurcheval.com/en/history/ferdinand-chevals-letter.html.

Grosz, Stephen. *The Examined Life: How We Lose and Find Ourselves*. Vintage Digital, 2013. Kindle edition.

Kaplan, Frederick S. "Fibrodysplasia Ossificans Progressiva: An Historical Perspective." *Clinical Reviews in Bone and Mineral Metabolism* 3, nos. 3–4 (2005): 179–81. ifopa.org/what-is-fop/fop-skeleton.html.

Kaplan, Frederick S. "FOP Skeleton." International Fibrodysplasia Ossificans Progressiva Association. Accessed June 8, 2016. http://www.ifopa.org/what-is-fop/fop-skeleton.html.

Leroi, Armand Marie. *Mutants: On Genetic Variety and the Human Body*. New York: Viking, 2003.

Lightman, Alan. *The Accidental Universe*. London: Constable, 2014.

Lorr, Benjamin. *Hell-Bent: Obsession, Pain, and the Search for Something Like Transcendence in Competitive Yoga*. New York: St. Martin's Press, 2012.

MacFarquhar, Larissa. "Last Call." *The New Yorker*, June 24, 2013. newyorker.com/magazine/2013/06/24/last-call-3.

Mansfield, Katherine. *The Collected Stories*. Introduction by Ali Smith. London: Penguin Classics, 2007.

Memory and Desire. Directed by Niki Caro. New Zealand: Frame Up Films, 1999.

O'Hara, Frank. "Adieu to Norman, Bon Jour to Joan and Jean-Paul." In *Collected Poems*, edited by Donald Allen. Berkeley and Los Angeles: University of California Press, 1995, 328.

"Our War Secret Exposed." *Taranaki Daily News*, February 16, 2009. stuff.co.nz/taranaki-daily-news/811650/our-war-secret-exposed.

"Phantom Black Dogs." Mysterious Britain and Ireland: Mysteries, Legends and the Paranormal. Accessed June 11, 2016. mysteriousbritain.co.uk/folklore/phantom-black-dogs.html.

Saitō, Tamaki. *Hikikomori: Adolescence Without End*. Translated by Jeffrey Angles. Minneapolis: University of Minnesota Press, 2013.

Shafritz, B., et al. "Overexpression of an Osteogenic Morphogen in Fibrodysplasia Ossificans Progressiva." *New England Journal of Medicine* 335, no. 8 (August 22, 1996): 555–61. nejm.org/doi/full/10.1056/NEJM199608223350804#t=articleTop.

Shore, Eileen M. "Fibrodysplasia Ossificans Progressiva (FOP): A Human Genetic Disorder of Extra-Skeletal Bone Formation, or, How Does One Tissue Become Another?" *Wiley Interdisciplinary Reviews: Developmental Biology* 1, no. 1 (2012): 153–65. ncbi.nlm.nih.gov/pmc/articles/ PMC3297114/.

Walrond, Carl. "Stewart Island/Rakiura: Stewart Island Places: North and West." *Te Ara—The Encyclopedia of New Zealand*. Last modified May 12, 2015. TeAra.govt.nz/en/stewart-islandrakiura/page-5.

Wells, Peter. "Of Memory and Desire." *Dangerous Desires*. Auckland: Reed, 1991.

Wolf, Michael. *Tokyo Compression*. Berlin: Peperoni Books, 2010. photomichaelwolf.com/#tokyo-compression/1.

Year Zero. Airwig Records. 2001, compact disc.

Young, JP. *Anniversary Day*. 2012, compact disc. jpyoung.bandcamp.com/album/anniversary-day.

Young, JP. *Jilted*. 2006, compact disc. jpyoung.bandcamp.com/album/jilted.

Young, JP. *The Te Kūiti Underground*. 2008, compact disc. jpyoung.bandcamp.com/album/the-te-kuiti-underground.

Zielenziger, Michael. *Shutting Out the Sun: How Japan Created Its Own Lost Generation*. New York: Random House, 2006.